MUMBAI V/S COVID

Joyking Birje

Notion Press Media Pvt Ltd

No. 50, Chettiyar Agaram Main Road,
Vanagaram, Chennai, Tamil Nadu – 600 095

First Published by Notion Press 2021
Copyright © Joyking Birje 2021
All Rights Reserved.

ISBN 978-1-68538-312-1

Disclaimer

The nature of this topic, makes it impossible to refrain from analysing, presenting facts, praising and sometimes criticising the Government, where necessary. When I say 'Government', it implies the people who are responsible for good governance to us across verticals. Not State v/s Center, or Right Wing v/s Left wing debates. I 'do' have very strong political opinions of my own. However, I assure you that I haven't allowed my personal preferences or opinions to dictate this books direction.

Contents

About the Author

The author, Mr. Joyking Birje is an educationalist by profession, socialist at heart, a family man by nature and loves to follow sports and travel in his leisure.

After completing his Honours from Mumbai University, he pursued his Masters in Human Resources, because that is where he believes the country's true future lies. He is also a certified Psychological counsellor. He has juggled between various reputed domestic and International Hospitality and Aviation companies, before settling down and realising his life-long dream of being an educator.

In his own words, he says the '*Shloka*' that has touched him the most and inspired his career path is:

"Gurur Brahma Gurur Vishnu

Gurur Devo Maheshwara

Guru Sakshat Parabrahma

Tasmai Shri Gurave Namah"

Joyking and his wife Reena, who are both equally passionate about their work, are the Founders of 'The National Institute of Hospitality and Aviation Management', an Institute with multiple branches in Mumbai and catering to Pan India students. They've successfully nurtured the careers of thousands of aspiring candidates in this sector all over the world.

Joyking has received numerous awards and recognitions for his work in the field of education pertaining to the hospitality and aviation industry. He has regularly been featured and interviewed regarding his work in leading local and national publications like The Mid-Day, Business Today, The Times of India, The Economic Times, etc. to name a few. He has also recently, on 28th July 2021 been awarded as 'Times Most Influential Person' in the category of Education, Aviation, by the country's No.1 Media Group, The Times Group of India.

While he has successfully written many academic books before, this is his first foray into mainstream Non-Fiction writing.

Acknowledgements and a Note for My Readers

Hi there! If you're reading this, it means you've probably bought a copy of my book. Thank you for that. Not just for buying/borrowing the book, but for giving me something invaluable in return – your time. I promise I'll try making it worth your while.

The purpose of me writing this book is crystal clear in my mind. Allow me to share it with you. This pandemic has changed me as a person and made me more socially active/responsible. I now understand that along with my privileges, I also have my duties towards my countrymen. If I can motivate even a handful of people to see my point of view, to become more socially responsible and ask for political accountability, I'd feel that my book is successful.

First, I'd like to thank Lord Shiva, for giving me the strength and vision to start the journey of writing this book. Also all the other gods. After all I'm a true Indian, so too many deities to name:). Let it suffice to say that

Lord Ram and Prophet Muhammad hold the same reverence in my eyes and heart.

Secondly, I'd like to thank the love of my life, my biggest support and my harshest critic, my wife Reena. She motivated me to write each page of this book, knowing that I'm a lazy bum who doesn't complete things. She also read each word that I have written and gave me her valuable inputs. Without her, this book truly wouldn't have happened.

Next, I'd like to thank my family, my extended family and my adorable nieces and nephew. They've always stood by me, given me unconditional love, and had the faith in me that I could do this. Thank you.

I would also like to thank Notion press and their excellent team for their absolute professional work. Especially my publishing Manager, Ms Yeshwini Doshi, who was constantly there to patiently answer all my queries and accept my numerous requests. Thanks!

Lastly, all my friends, in India and from across the world, my readers, people who connect with me on social media. You all have made my life a better place. A big heartfelt thanks to all of you. Let the journey begin.

Chapter 1
The First Wave

The city of dreams. India's financial capital. The city that never sleeps. The maximum City. MUMBAI. The city that I and millions like me call home. The city that is home to people from different cities and states. Students come here to study. Professionals, to make a career. Businessmen, to fulfil their dreams & migrant labourers to fill their stomachs. The city of Bollywood. This is a city with the tallest towers and the finest hotels. This is the city in which the Ambani's live in their monstrous 27 stories house Antilia. It is also the city with the largest slum in Asia, Dharavi.

11th March 2020. The day the saga began in Mumbai with only two confirmed cases. Cases started increasing at an alarming rate. Our PM Shri Narendra Modi announced a 'Janta Curfew' on 22nd March, so that the government could set up a task force to handle the challenges ahead. We were asked to stay indoors unless essential and clap our hands, light diyas or/and bang thalis in the evening.

This was just a start to a long series of extended lockdowns that ranged for a period starting from 23rd March till June.

So what's the big deal? The big deal is that Mumbai is made of a multi-cultural, diversely economic population as pointed earlier. Many earn their daily bread. Literally! They were left stranded on the road. Also, outside railway stations & bus stands. Once again, Literally! The world was watching how Mumbai dealt with the pandemic. This wasn't the picture it needed to see. There wasn't a news channel that wasn't streaming the plight of our visitors, our labourers, our workers, our domestic help, our friendly carpenter, plumber, restaurant waiter.

In its own capacity to contain the spread of COVID-19, the Maharashtra government put in place a series of restrictions in the days leading up to the March 24 nationwide lockdown. On March 20, Chief Minister Uddhav Thackeray imposed a lockdown in the Mumbai Metropolitan Region, Pune, Pimpri-Chinchwad and Nagpur until March 31. Suddenly, in just a few hours, lakhs of migrant workers living in the city found themselves without work. To make matters worse, there was little or no guarantee that they would get basic amenities such as food and water. This forced thousands of migrant labourers to flock to the city's major train termini — the Lokmanya Tilak Terminus and the Chhatrapati Shivaji Maharaj Terminus — as well as train and bus terminals in other cities. Following the Chief Minister's announcement, the Railways operated 14 special trains on March 20 and 21, eight of them from Mumbai, to various destinations such as Patna, Howrah, Danapur, Gorakhpur, Manduadih and Balharshah. Long-distance passenger services were initially shut only on March 22 on account of the Janata Curfew. However, the suspension of services was extended to March 31 and then to April 14 after the Prime Minister announced the lockdown. Shahrukh Malik, a driver of Ola and Uber cabs, said: "Had we known this was going to last this long, we would have gone home much earlier and returned after two-three months." Visuals of hundreds of workers wearing *gamchas,* carrying heavy backpacks and wailing children, and walking on national highways, boarding tractors, and jostling for space atop multi-coloured buses became defining images for days to come in India.

Pls allow me to tell you a few short stories.

1. On May 6th, 2020, NDTV spotted a group of 20 people walking from Ghansoli in Navi Mumbai to their village in Buldana. The group includes young children and a seven-month pregnant woman, all taking the journey by foot with little food and money. "I sit once in a while...," said Nikita, the pregnant woman, as she walked

on the road wearing a saree. The woman, who started her walk at 7 pm yesterday, said she had been on the road for the last 12 hours. A young man walked behind her, carrying their belongings on his head. "What will we do staying here? There are no arrangements here for our food and water, she said. The daily wage earners also fear the situation for them will worsen in cities once the monsoon sets in. "Once it starts raining here, it will be difficult to get food and water. When we go to the police station to seek permission, they beat us," the man walking behind her said. Another young woman was seen walking, carrying one child on her hips and the other, on her shoulder.

8:53 AM · May 6, 2020

2. In the rising heat, Goutam Lal Meena, a mason, had walked on uneven tar roads in his sandals. He said he had survived on water and biscuits. Work

and wages dried up after India declared a 21-day lockdown with four hours notice on the midnight of 24 March to prevent the spread of coronavirus. (India has reported more than 1,000 COVID-19 cases and 27 deaths so far.) The shutting down of all transport meant that he was forced to travel on foot.

"I walked through the day and I walked through the night. What option did I have? I had little money and almost no food," Mr Meena told me, his voice raspy and strained. - as reported in BBC News on 30th March 2020 by Soutik Biswas.

3. "In my 20 years in Mumbai, I have never seen such a sight," said Gopal Das as he recounted his ordeal on March 21 at the Lokmanya Tilak Terminus. Gopal was among the sea of people who had attempted to board what would be the last few trains out of the city to their homes hundreds of kilometres away. Gopal, a construction worker, did not manage to board the train. And nothing had prepared him for what was to follow. Gopal is from Bhagalpur, Bihar. He said he and his friends spent nearly four hours trying to get tickets. "A few people who had clambered on to the trains fell on the platform. A little later, we heard that all the trains had been cancelled. Since there was no

public transport, we walked for three hours to our room in Bandra (East) with ₹250 in our pockets. We were still hoping they would start the trains. We didn't think it would last this long," he said. - as reported in The Hindu April 4th 2020.

4. A pregnant migrant labourer, who was walking from Maharashtra to Madhya Pradesh in the lockdown, delivered a baby on the road. She then walked for another 150 kilometres. Luckily for her, they survived.

5. A group of 16 migrants from Madhya Pradesh who were walking back from Maharashtra, were run over by a goods train when they fell asleep on the railway tracks after being exhausted after the long walk. Guess their luck was asleep too, just like our government.

6. I know a skilled and cheerful carpenter Pintu. He had moved his shared rental accommodation from a shanty in Bandra East to a slum in Vasai as the rent was far cheaper. They were a bunch of immigrants from the same village of U.P. He called once every week to check if online train bookings had started. Once, some local politician, tried to incite immigrants by asking them to arrive at Bandra terminus.

Mumbai's Bandra stationed witnessed a large crowd on Tuesday as migrant workers hoping to get back home gathered there (India Today photo)

Did any political party actually care for these migrants? I find it hard to believe so. In fact they were more concerned on playing blame games. Here's a tweet thats laughable. Laughable because the incident was happening a stone throw distance away from our Cabinet Minister Shri Aaditya Thackeray's home.

I would like to clarify that I hold Aaditya Thackeray in the highest regards. I believe Aaditya really cares about this city, is a visionary and in the days to come is going to be instrumental in transforming Mumbai to a 24/7 city. A city that never sleeps. A city that is clean and safe. Not just modern, he is also restoring all the old pyaus and old monuments that are important footprints of our heritage. I've written this, to clarify that I'm not using this book to malign any political figure. Nor to glorify anyone. Just state facts.

This tweet was just one of the many incidents that reflected the helplessness of those in power to do anything, absolutely *NOTHING* for the people who make up the *REAL* Mumbai. Our lifeline. And also testament to something that I will repeat a zillion times. This was an ill planned lockdown. Period.

So the only option left was to shift blame and protect self image! And not just this, everything became a blame game. Instead of strengthening our own medical infrastructure, increasing testing centres, preferably in every alternate pin code, the media were busy showing politicians calling COVID-19 as Wuhan Virus or Chinese virus and feel happy about it! Yes, we dislike China at some level. Yes, we want Asian supremacy. But seriously, I mean, *WTF* is there to be happy where the virus bloody originated from if it's your own people who are dying? Body counts were being declared non-stop across all news channels like some cricket scores. They just kept getting bad. Then, worse. Hundred's somewhere, thousands somewhere else. I shudder when I remember the fact that all these numbers are fake and grossly under reported. Human deaths had become a number that were being updated daily.

These poor innocents ran in despair, hoping that at last their suffering would end. At least SOMEONE cared for them. They were sent back after a full days begging, crying, media circus & political drama. It was the next day that it occurred to me that I never even asked Pintu if he needed any help. He was jobless for 3 months. I called, he humbly asked if i could transfer 2000 to his account as they were out of rations. I transferred 5000 immediately and asked him to count on me for any monetary assistance until he safely returned home. I'm attaching an image of the chat with him to prove authenticity of this event.

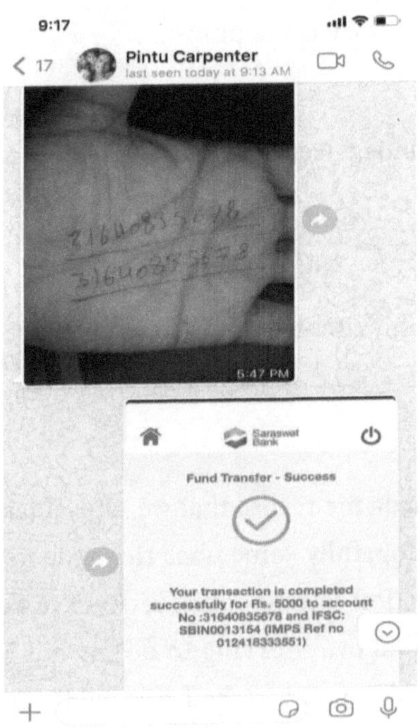

Now, some of you might question my intentions of writing the last story, correct?

Sounds like a show-off?

Let me assure you, the answer is NO. (Had i wanted to show-off, the amount would've been higher!)

There are a million of stories out there on the internet and news that you have already read and seen. Men walking with all their belongings on their backs, women walking with their kids on their chest and heads. People crying. You don't need me to tell you more stories of misery. That's not the purpose of this book.

The sixth story is the purpose.

"Zindagi jeene ke do hi tarike hote hai-

Ek, jo ho raha hai hone do,

Bardaasht karte jao,

Ya phir zimmedari uthao use badalne ki."

– Rang De Basanti

Pintu made me realise that we, the educated middle-class, (and hopefully some uber rich readers too) have a moral obligation towards our society. I've dedicated the last year and above in trying to do my bit. My wife told me that many employers had not paid our maid for 3 months of lockdown as they weren't allowed to visit our society. Is that fair? How will they feed their families? My family did what we could and beyond. Gave salary, loans and rations. Ditto to the domestic help of the offices. We tried to spread awareness amongst friends & society about the same.

Yes, the government whom we have voted into power failed us. Yes, they are answerable to us. The time to ask questions will come. Once the dust settles there will be accountability. *If* we stand united.

But until than, it is we, the citizens, along with the help of any willingly helpful government department (eg. BMC), caring local or state level politician (you will be surprised how many good ones actually exist) social activists (Mumbai is blessed with loads of angels) and the goodness within our soul that can save our homeland.

And that, my dear readers, is what sets Mumbai apart. The sheer number of volunteers, NGO's, social workers and just normal good hearted Samaritans that came out to help those who needed it the most was phenomenal.

Now let's recount the events that preluded all this. The Government announced lockdown and shut shops. Period. Moratoriums were granted on loan repayments and free rations and meagre cash were announced to a small percentage of the population. There were cries for food from hungry families. Families that the people in power couldn't (wouldn't?) reach. Thats where numerous NGO's helped. Far too many to name. One that I would name, simply because I was and still am a part of is Khaana Chahiye, founded by Ruben Mascarenhas along with Swaraj Shetty and his team, as a fight against hunger. What started as a small scale food delivery helping hand is now a large scale food & ration SOS delivering NGO that has reached out to thousands of households across Mumbai, Thane & MMR. They provide 10 k daily meals to the homeless. There are many such NGO's in the city who are doing their bit. Another one that I know closely is Withaarya charitable trust, founded by Shital Bhatkar, which has done some absolutely amazing work. Kudos to them and all the other unnamed godsends who prove the age old saying that Mumbai is not just a name, it's an emotion!

In fact, Amit Shah acknowledged this. To quote him "Non-governmental organisations helped people in all possible ways. When migrants were going back home, NGOs provided them food, water, shelter and helped them reach their destinations. The government could not have done it all alone," he said. My question is, why? Why the government couldn't have done it all alone? Are they short of funds? Manpower? Vehicles? Rations? State and Centre co-ordination? Or simply the will power? If that is the case, I beg to ask the question how was this lockdown any different from the emergency declared in 1975 by the then PM Indira Gandhi? Just by calling it Janta Lockdown doesn't wash the establishments hands clean of its responsibilities!

Another bone of contention that I would like to point out is the sheer number of Indians who were stuck abroad and not being brought back! Yes, in spite of what the GOI has been telling us, no, they did not bring everyone home. Yeah, maybe from the U.S.A. or Australia and Europe. But what about places like U.A.E.? I personally have so many friends and relatives who were stuck there for three months. Initially they were told it's just a lockdown for a week to 10 days so they decided to complete their work and then return. But then the lockdown got extended! They lost their jobs! Some of them were small time workers with meagre earnings! Some were well to do, like my brother-in-law who has his own residence and so sustenance wasn't an issue. But everyone wasn't so lucky. People were literally queuing outside the Indian embassy and being shunned! Even after 3 months, when flights resumed, they were mostly to Kerala, almost none to Mumbai! So some guys chartered a flight back home. Is this how our government treats our citizens? That too at such times? Despicable!

In the meanwhile the price of a test could not exceed the upper limit set by the Indian Council for Medical Research: Rs 4,500 in May 2020 (source indiatoday.in) This, in a pandemic. Forgive me if I sound naive here, but shouldn't the government be conducting tests left right and center to identify any case as early as possible? Shouldn't our government be responsible for testing costs since it's a damn pandemic for crying out loud!

So, my dear readers, you can imagine the gross undermining of the number of tests been actually done, since most of the population wouldn't or couldn't afford to pay the money, nor face the fear and uncertainty of treatment!

Bodies were piling up in mortuaries and the city's densest slum, Dharavi, was battling a fast growing coronavirus crisis. Our Chief Minister Shri Uddhav Thackeray handed over the reins of BMC to Municipal Commissioner Iqbal Singh Chahal. His team went door to door in Dharavi looking for people with symptoms and eventually isolating 150,000 people from the slum, a move that stopped the chain of infection. At the time, Chahal also abolished the central hub handling the city's crisis and created local war rooms in each of the 24 administrative divisions — wards or neighbourhoods of the city.

Other areas too were affected similarly. Entire zones were declared as contamination zones and sealed. Every effort was made to curb the pandemic from spreading out of control. Mumbai is the world's second-most densely packed city, according to data from the United Nations. About 32,000 people are crammed in per square kilometre. It's no mean feat to control something of this magnitude. In that regards, hats off to the BMC, Mumbai Police, Health care workers, NGO's & activists. I salute you all. Mumbai shall forever remain indebted to you.

People were hiding in their homes if they felt even the slightest symptoms of COVID-19, until they recovered through sheer luck and locally obtained medicines or till they grew incurably ill. So, while we all were conveniently in lockdown, some random numbers were forced down our throats, while our Prime Minister blew success trumpets about how India has defeated Covid and life resumed to normal! I had once read somewhere that a true Diplomat is someone who can tell you to go to hell in such a way that you actually look forward to the trip. Get the hint;)

Speaking about our PM, there is also this small matter of the PM cares Fund which was launched on27[th] March 2020, following the -19 pandemic in India. But more about that in the second chapter.

Chapter 2

Callousness

Thank you for staying with me till the second chapter. So we now have reached the stage where the whole country, Mumbai in particular was at least partially to largely unlocked. The Chief Minister's COVID-19 Relief Fund in Maharashtra received a whopping Rs 342 crore in donations till around mid-May. Of this, 23.82 crore had been spent on controlling the virus's spread, while Rs 55.20 crore went towards facilitating the journey of migrant workers, an RTI inquiry revealed. And yeah, remember the 16 labourers who died sleeping on the railway tracks? Their families were compensated Rs. 5 lakhs each.

Now let's move on to the mysterious PM Cares (Does he?) fund. As mentioned earlier it was launched on 27th March 2020, following the COVID-19 pandemic in India. The stated purpose of the fund was to combat and contain. Period. (Please note there already exists a PM's National relief Fund PMNRF to provide relief and assistance to those suffering in times of natural disasters and calamities). But NAMO is larger than life. He wanted his own project. Different rules. No accountability. No Right to Information (RTI) act. Foreign donations accepted without scrutiny by Foreign Contribution Regulation Act 2010 (FCRA). What did you say? Right, Modi Hai, Toh Mumkin hain!

"People from all walks of life expressed their desire to donate to India's war against COVID-19. Respecting that spirit, the Prime Minister's Citizen Assistance and Relief in Emergency Situations Fund has been constituted. This will go a long way in creating a healthier India," Prime minister's first tweet said.

PM added that the PM-CARES Fund accepts micro-donations too and that was meant to further strengthen disaster management capacities and encourage research on protecting citizens. (I repeat 'ENCOURAGE RESEARCH')

"Let us leave no stone unturned to make India healthier and more prosperous for our future generations," he tweeted.

Bollywood actor Akshay Kumar was among the first to announce a donation to the fund. PM tagged his tweet where he pledged Rs 25 crore to the cause.

From March 27-31, 2020, in just 4 days Rs 3,076.62 crore was collected under PM CARES Fund, according to the official website. The fund has been come under criticism for its lack of transparency regarding the usage of contributions.

The Supreme Court on August 18 refused to order the transfer of money under the PM CARES fund to the National Disaster Relief Fund (NDRF). That cleared the way for Shri Narendra Modi to do anything he pleased with the funds. He could buy golden NAMO masks if he wanted to;) Thankfully for us, he didn't!

I know I sound spiteful at times. That's because I love my country, my state, my city & all human beings in general (It obviously goes without saying that I do reserve prejudice & judgement towards some who do not deserve to be loved). The official page of PM cares fund said that the funds will be used for availability of quality treatment and encourage research on ways to beat coronavirus. THIS IS WHERE WE WERE LET DOWN/ FAILED/CHEATED.

The rest of the educated world, the Americans, Europeans and others were investing heavily in research for vaccines. In the mean time they were also sponsoring research in other countries and placing bulk orders for the same in advance.

What did our government do?

They told us research is going fine. Invested peanuts compared to the astronomical funds collected in the PM cares fund on research and procurement of vaccines. And they did this all the while knowing very well about our large population and concentrated cities! Hell, our PM even declared on television that India will be a superpower due to vaccine manufacturing! Instead of diving head first into vaccine procurement, collaborations with manufacturers, funding Serum Institute of India and Bharat Infotech with huge amounts of money and also joining hands with promising foreign manufacturers, India moved about as if all was well. Yes, I won't deny that some work was being done at various levels. But those were baby steps for crying out loud! The country needed more. The states, cities, all needed more. The rich and poor alike. People from Delhi, Bihar, Guwahati, Jaipur & Mumbai alike. We all needed more.

Instead of demanding accountability from the ones in power, the media circus was busier in Sushant Singh Rajput's case. Not that it didn't deserve coverage. But not as much as it actually got. And then the responsible journalists fed us with every tiny detail of Rhea's daily life (and her family's). Then the drug's scandal of Bollywood. All matters of far more importance than a raging pandemic that could unleash a second wave anytime.

All this while, there was almost no appropriate behaviour being followed. Crowds in Mumbai local trains have always been a subject of folklore.

Over 26 lakh passengers travelled in Mumbai locals on the first day after service resumes for all. (Forget the ticketless ones;)) This was on February 1st 2021.

(Photo: PTI)

UPDATED: February 1, 2021 23:34 IST

Mumbai local train services resumed for general public on February 1. (Photo: PTI)

So, obviously all kinds of appropriate behaviour, 1 metre distance rule, social distancing, not rubbing your bodies against each other, not coughing on each others faces and such niceties as you might imagine went for a toss. The same happened throughout the country. So was starting normal life wrong? Am I advocating people sitting at home and not earning their livelihoods? A BIG RESOUNDING NO!

All that I'm trying to say is that the time available from when the first wave started, from when the PM Cares fund was launched, till the time all metropolitan cities in the country were opened 100% was more than adequate to set up the required medical infrastructure to cope up and fight with the inevitable impending second wave head-on. We had the money. We had the doctors. We had the infrastructure. We had every conceivable resource that could focus on the main areas of concern which were bound to be badly affected. All that we lacked was the vision and the will power. And this from the government which for the first time in our history is unanimously celebrated as the best. This model, that model, my stinky commode. No sir, we failed as a country. No state, No centre. One country. India. It wasn't Delhites who died, nor Mumbaikars or Biharis. They were all Indians. Their miseries boiled down to just one simple word. CALLOUSNESS.

Chapter 3

The Inevitable Second Wave

Thank you once again for continuing with me in this journey through the third chapter. If you recollect in the last chapter we read about how Mumbai local trains went live from 1st February 2021. We all know by now that Delhi and Mumbai are the two most strong case studies about how efficiently (or inefficiently, based on how you prefer perceiving it) medical infrastructures were handled. To bring things into perspective, I'd like to share a graph with my readers.

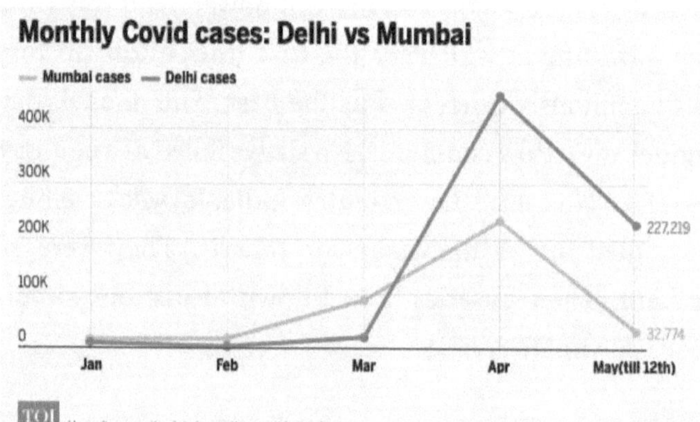

So, as you see above, the cases of in Mumbai spiked almost immediately after the local trains went live, validating the point I made earlier. Whereas in Delhi, the second wave took a month longer to start. This is a clear indicator that the starting of local trains in Mumbai brought on the second wave.

But thankfully, this time round Mumbai was at least better prepared than the 1st wave. Not completely prepared by any stretch of imagination, I assure you, but definitely better prepared. For example, during the first wave, temporary hospitals had been set up by the team of Mumbai's Municipal Commissioner Iqbal Singh Chahal. They weren't dismantled in Mumbai even when the cases dipped. Another very interesting thing is that unlike most Indian hospitals that relied on cylinders, they had been equipped with pipes that supplied oxygen directly to patients' beds. This proved to be a masterstroke.

Lets take a real live example. At midnight on April 17' 2021, as a deadly new wave of the coronavirus overwhelmed India, Iqbal Singh Chahal learned that six hospitals in his city would run out of oxygen within hours — putting the lives of 168 patients at risk. The patients were immediately rushed to the temporary hospitals that you just read about. All 168 survived.

This is the sort of preparation that chapter 2 referred to. This is what can be the difference between life and death. Delhi, unfortunately, were lagging far too behind. As of May 11' 2021, Mumbai had almost half the number of active virus cases as capital New Delhi. I won't get into Delhi's mismanagement, political games, the lack of beds or oxygen supply, because this book is to talk about Mumbai. That discussion is for another day.

Still, the risks to Mumbai are far from over. The city has recorded 688,696 cases since the pandemic began, adding 1,544 on May 16' 2021. Chahal is preparing for a third wave by setting up jumbo paediatric hospitals because public health experts have warned his team that more children might be infected in the next surge.

Managing the spread of the virus in Mumbai is of paramount importance not just for the city, but also for the country. Simply because Mumbai is India's financial capital. The countries GDP is already crippling. The less spoken about the Finance budget allocation and their decision on not printing new notes the better. Let the economists decide how screwed up we already are. God forbid if Mumbai comes to a long time stand still, the countries economy will go for a further downward spiral. We simply can't afford that. Not now, not for the next 10 years at least!

Maharashtra CM announced another lockdown in the second week of April, it should have been announced one month earlier, says Dr AvinashBhondwe (As published on June 8th 2021, Hindustan times).

In February and March, it was noticed that…

- ▲ Numbers are increasing rapidly

- ▲ Symptoms are changing. Low-grade fever, severe breathlessness, loose motions, vomiting, rashes over the body, tongue, and anosmia were the new symptoms.

- ▲ The upper middle-class and elite in big housing societies and bungalows outnumbered the slum dwellers in getting infected

- ▲ The age group of 20 to 45 years was mainly affected

- ▲ A large number of children below 10 years of age were getting infected

This was the beginning of the Second Wave. Doctors and scientists informed the government of Maharashtra that this is the second wave and a new mutant of Maharashtra origin has surfaced. Government of Maharashtra clearly said that there is no second wave and no mutants.

It was Rajesh Bhushan, chief secretary of health, Central government who finally, on March 24, 2021, conveyed to the Maharashtra government the existence of the mutant of - B.1.617.1 and B.1.617.2, and also declared that it is the second wave.

Bhushan pointed out and the doctors in the state said that:

- Contact tracing of 30 testings per new patient is required.

- Considering the massive rise in the number of patients, the need to make necessary infrastructure arrangements was stressed, but these suggestions were not followed.

During this second wave, Maharashtra was India's worst-affected state, just as it was in the first wave of COVID-19 last year.

As of April 27, Maharashtra had 676,647 active patients, almost a quarter of the national total of 2,882,204. The state has so far recorded more than 0.1 million deaths, 30 percent of the national total of 3,46,000.

Data with the Maharashtra health department shows that the growth of positive cases had been exponential since February 12, which the state marks as the start of the second wave.

Maharashtra recorded 2,052,905 cases in the 11 months between March 9, 2020, and February 11, 2021. Then in just the first 72 days of the second wave, between February 12 and April 25 — it recorded 2,174,654 cases. Almost 70 percent of these cases have been recorded in Tier II, Tier III cities, and the villages.

These are just numbers. In my opinion, grossly under reported. Not in Mumbai to a large extent, maybe, but I would go out on a limb here to bet the overall numbers of Maharashtra is a joke. Even so, we are far better off than some other states, for example Kerala, who declared a positivity rate of 10% in the peak. That was laughable to say the least. It only meant gross under-testing and un-reporting of cases and that no one gives a damn because Kerala is ruled by CPM.

BBC News had reported on 20th November' 2020 that in Kerala, a team led by Dr Arun N Madhavan, a general medicine physician, they checked the district editions of seven local newspapers and followed five news channels unfailingly every day. They took notes on every death reported in the news and obituary notices and diligently entered the details in a spreadsheet. The volunteers had counted 3,356 deaths from the infection in Kerala. But the official death toll from the disease is 1,969.

Similarly, it was reported after thorough investigation in Parts of Gujarat like Ahmedabad, where bodies were counted in excess of 200 per night, but official figures released were only 25! On a night in Vadodara a single newspaper counted more than 83 deaths, but the next morning the official figure was only 13! That is the level of incompetence (if you prefer using that word. I prefer lies.)

Murky politics!

Sorry for diverting from Mumbai, but this was necessary to get an idea that although we were doing bad, we were far better than most cities/states in the country. At least we didn't have bodies floating in the holy Ganges and so called 'journalists' thinking that was all there was left to report about to the international media about a country with a population of 1.4 billion (discounting the illegal immigrants).

There was a shortage of medical oxygen even in the first wave in October 2020. But the government did not improve production and remained happy with 1,200 metric tonnes per day.

In April, during the peak period, the requirement escalated to 3,000 metric tonnes per day. Even with all the additional support, like the "Oxygen Express" train, the situation did not improve in time.

Around 40 per cent of the deaths that occurred in March and April 2021, were because of a lack of oxygen.

This is where the real problem lies. The great freedom fighter Chandrashekhar Azad had said:

"Ab bhi jiska khoon na khaula, khoon nahin woh paani hain,

Jo desh ke kaam na aaye, woh bekaar jawaani hain."

It is insignificant whether the wrong doer is a foreign tyrant invader like the Mughals or British, or if it's our own elected body. India doesn't need rulers. We don't need dictatorship. We need honest hardworking caring people who 'Govern' us. Hence, the term 'Government', not 'Maharaj'". India is a young country. We need to stand up, raise our voices and make sure it is heard.

Large-scale use of the impure industrial oxygen, along with unhygienic practices at hospitals is a probable cause of post- complications, like the Mucormycosis infection. This number has reached 11,000 cases.

Here's another interesting figure. 75% of adults speak negatively about Math. 44% HATE Math! (I checked Google, *baba*!) So my dear readers, I apologise for throwing so many numbers and statistics at you. I realise it's boring as hell to most of you. *2 lac cases this, 70% positivity rate that and what not.* By that account, this chapter hands down is boring, right?;)

But please change the way you look at this for a moment. These are NOT numbers. These are people. Real, living, working, family *wallahs*. Just like you and me. Both rich and poor. Both young and old. Many of them survived. Many didn't. Out of those who didn't, a survey revealed most were sole bread earners of their family. So it isn't only one life (or number), but the future of the entire family. Their children's education. In some cases, even survival.

At the peak, people were getting admitted in hospitals and many were coming out in body bags. There were 6 hour long queues at some crematoriums. Reminds me of the long queues of people standing outside banks and ATM's after demonetisation in 2016. Another blotch in our history.

So let's not get bored looking at these numbers. Let's not get happy that the death rate in Mumbai is reducing. The other day someone told me that the death count is just 21 today. *JUST 21*? Seriously? What if one of those 21 were someone you knew, cared about deeply, or worse, a family member? I'm sorry, but we NEED to care. We NEED to feel others loss. It's what makes us human beings. (Even animals mourn the loss of their kind)

Let these numbers serve as an eye opener for appropriate behaviour and getting ourselves vaccinated at the first available opportunity.

The official death count as of end-June 2021 is 400,000. That's a joke.

In a research conducted by the Center for Global Development which was published by The Indian Express, there were three different methods used to reach close to a fair number of actual cases. The entire study, if you wish to read is available online on their website. I'll just present the table to you that shows the stark difference between actual deaths in the first and second wave due to against official counts.

Table. Estimates of All-Cause Excess Mortality (millions)

Data Source/methodology	Wave 1 (May 2020 - March 2021)	Wave 2 (April 2021 – May/June 2021)	Total
1.States' Civil Registration Systems (CRS)	2	1.4	3.4
2.Indian sero-prevalence surveys plus international age-specific infection fatality rates	1.5	2.4	4.0
3.Consumer Pyramid Household Survey (CPHS) of CMIE	3.4	1.5	4.9
Official	0.16	0.24	0.4

In the meanwhile, while dealing with the pandemic we had people proclaiming Gaumutra as a cure for. *(I do not wish to hurt religious sentiments here. I practice Hinduism myself, among other religions, and understand the significance of Gaumutra. However, the fact remains, it's no cure for COVID-19)* We had self proclaimed 'Baba' Ramdev come up with some joke of a medicine that boosts immunity and cures COVID-19. We had election rallies *(Didi O Didi!)* and *'kumbhmela'* with thousands of people on the roads.

We can ill afford such behaviour. In fact there needs to be a law passed with severe penalties including jail time for such people. Including those who hold government offices. And religious heads or baba's. It is because of these dumb/evil people that the pandemic has spread further, taken more lives, and innocent people are forced to suffer lockdowns. Here's an image of the famous Kumbhmela:

ANI ✔ @ANI · 11/04/21

#WATCH Devotees in large numbers gathered at Har ki Pauri today ahead of Ganga aarti, in Haridwar

'Shahi Snan' scheduled to be held on 12th and 14th April during Haridwar Kumbh #Uttarakhand

651K views

 1,065    2,752    6,575

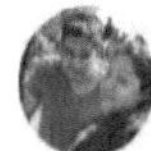

joyking @the_joyking · 12/04/21

Abhi yeh sab chalega???!!! This isn't anti national? Than why were we crying from our rooftops against Tablighi Jamaats?? @narendramodi @PMOIndia @aajtak @BJP4India

In fact, on July 16' 2021, the Supreme court had to once again intervene and teach the government common sense. Health and the Right to Life is paramount, the Supreme Court said, as it gave the Uttar Pradesh government two days time to reconsider its decision to allow the Kanwar Yatra this year amid worries.

"We all are citizens of India. Article 21 - the Right to Life - applies to all. UP cannot go ahead with physical yatra. 100 percent," said Justice RF Nariman.

Posting the next hearing to Monday, the Supreme Court said it was giving the state "one more opportunity to reconsider" or else, it would pass orders. Thankfully, the yatra was cancelled. The Supreme Court probably saved the lives of thousands of devotees and lakhs of Indians with just one judgement. A judgement that in the first place should've been taken by the government. If it had the *intent* to save lives.

So as the cases started rising Maharashtra Chief Minister Uddhav Thackeray on Tuesday announced a "mini lockdown" in the State for 15 days from 8 p.m. on Wednesday, 14th April 2021. According to the guidelines announced by the State government, Section 144 would be imposed for 15 days and no one would be allowed to move in public places without valid reason.

All establishments, public places, activities and services would remain closed. Only services and activities mentioned under 'essential category' would be exempted.

Private vehicles can run on the roads only for emergency services. All previous directions regarding the closure of theatres, malls, salons and swimming pools are to continue. Any residential co-operative society with more than five active coronavirus positive cases will be treated as a micro-containment zone.

However, one MAJOR difference between the lockdown in the first wave and this was that there were no bank moratoriums granted on loans. Hence, the middle class, many of whom had lost their jobs were in a mess. Also shop owners, small businessmen, and countless people who couldn't earn in their lockdown. Think about them. Their rents, home loans, other loans, household expenses, utility bills, children's fees (although education was online, all schools charged full fees as per offline norms. Even though they saved electricity, maintenance & other such costs!). Some families had savings. They managed. Some didn't have savings, they plunged into financial poverty.

The Indian middle class shrunk by a record 32 million due to COVID-19 pandemic downturns, according to an analysis by the US based Pew Research Center. This accounts for 60 per cent of the global retreat in the middle income tier. YES, you read that correctly. 60% of the people in the whole bloody world who shrunk from the middle class to poverty are Indians. *Let that sink in.* What a shame. What did our government do for them. This could've been avoided had the vaccination drive, when it was started, not been a complete joke. But that's for the next chapter.

All the blame doesn't lie solely with bad governance. It's also we, the public who have to share responsibility. As soon as things get a little better, people start rushing off to tourist hotspots like Lonavala, Goa, Manali, etc.

Huge crowds. Temporary boost of tourism and jobs for nearby villagers as waiters, housekeeping staff, cooks, etc. This in turn causes a spike in numbers causing a further lockdown. More job losses. A lot of them return to their cities or villages infected with or worse with a new mutation. We know by now that the virus is mutating rapidly. There is the dangerous Delta variant. It reportedly spreads faster than chickenpox. Also, it can easily be passed on by completely vaccinated people. There is also a worse new Lambda variant.

If we do not stop this irresponsible behaviour and unnecessary travelling, crowding and any sort of inappropriate behaviour than this epidemic will never end. Simply because the current vaccines haven't been tested as efficient against the emerging new mutations. People will continue dying. Worse still, others for no fault of their own will continue being forced into lockdown.

A key problem faced by the poor and strangely in some cases even middle-class families was getting enough rations to feed themselves on a daily basis. Daily labourers, coolies, and many others who come in the 'daily wage' category were dumped. The government couldn't help all. People were starving. Horribly and despicably so.

There is this song *'Doori'* in the fantastic movie *'Gully Boy'* that aptly describes the situation here:

Koi mujhko ye bataaye

Kyun ye doori aur majboori

Iss duniya ki kya story

Kiske haath mein iski dori

Right mein building aasmanoko chhuri

Left mein bacchii bhookhi sadko pe so ri

Kaisi yeh majboori paisa rehna hai zaroori

Nahi to kaise hogi poori teri seena-zori

Lambi gaadi jitni kiski kholi

Haan chawal ki khali bori

Ek paiso se bhari poori

Kaisi ye majboori, haan?

Bolna!

Ab dekho toh hum paas lekin

Socho kitni doori hai

Ab kaisi yeh majboori hai

Socho kitni doori hai!

We need to decrease this '*doori*'. We, the privileged need to reach out to them and do anything and everything that we can within our own individual capacity to help them out. Maybe a meal? Some rations? A job? Milk and biscuits for the kids? Sanitary equipment to fight the pandemic like masks, hand wash, soaps, sanitizers, etc. The list is endless. It's the *will* that we need to create. If you remember in chapter 1, I mentioned about how my carpenter *Pintu* made me realise that I do have a moral obligation towards society. That is when I started doing all that I could manage. For humans and animals. Along with my wife, the kindest human I know, Reena. We spent money from our own accounts as well as did volunteer work wherever necessary. The work we did with NGO Khaanachahiye remains very close to my heart. But the closest, something that I'll cherish forever, is when my Management Institute, NIHAM, started involving our students and doing charity work. We sponsored rations, meal packets, etc. And asked our students to distribute them to the needy. It was great to see these young adults feel the happiness of giving, of helping the needy. Something that will serve our society well in the future.

Awesome work with Khaanachahiye:

Khaana Chahiye ✔ @kha… · 16/05/21 ⋯
At @mybmc 's request @khaanachahiye will be supporting 5000 meals for lunch and dinner, starting tomorrow, for the next 3 days for all those who have been evacuated, from coastal areas in Mumbai and are presently in shelters.

#CycloneTauktae

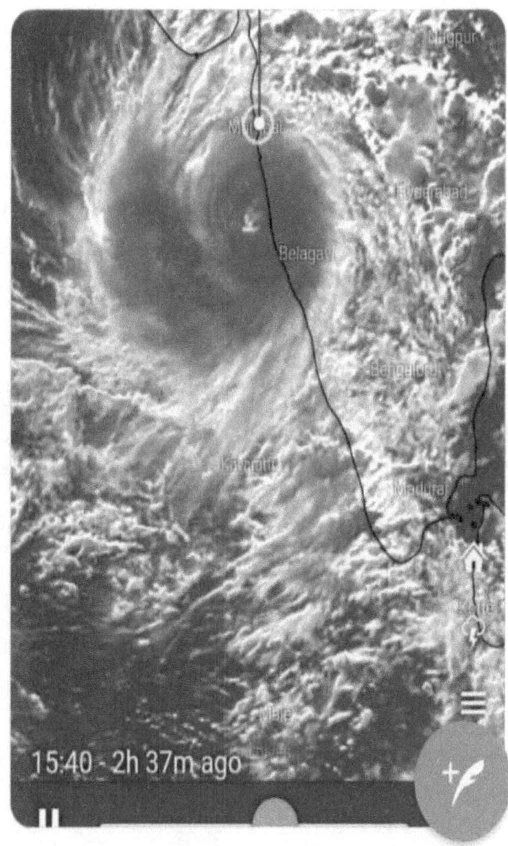

mint_lounge @Mint_Lounge · 25/05/21 ···

. @khaanachahiye, a Mumbai-based non-profit, has mobilised hundreds of #volunteers to continue #food aid beyond the pandemic. @Jahnabee writes. #CycloneTauktae

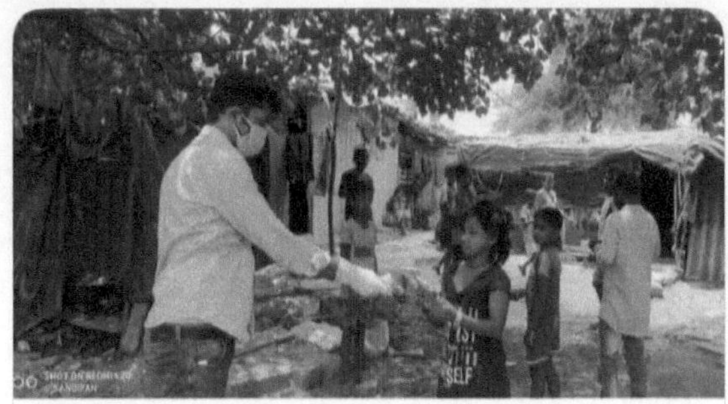

lifestyle.livemint.com
Cyclone Tauktae and how citizens fight hunger

Kanushree @Kanushree · 26/05/21 ···
Mumbai people any leads if we can help this lady? You can DM him if you do, he's in touch with her.
She's willing to work as a cook/ house staff fulltime in someone's home or any place that's in need of a cook. Apparently she's a great one! :)
Brugen is a fellow Covid volunteer!

BRUGEN @brugenrajan · 25/05/21

I know a lady who used to sell poha upma idli dosa to various offices. But due to lockdown & WFH of all the offices she is jobless now. Cooking is the only medium of income for her fa…

Show this thread

💬 3   🔁 1   ♡ 2   ↑

Ashu ✔ @AshwiniDodani · 26/05/21 ···
@khaanachahiye @rubenmasc anyway we can help?

💬 1   🔁   ♡ 1   ↑

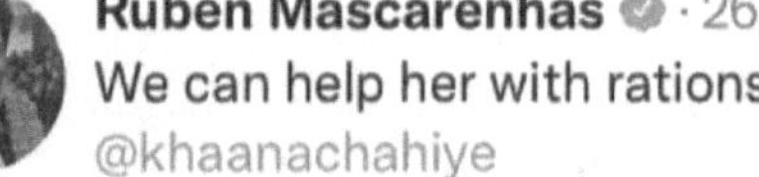

Ruben Mascarenhas ✔ · 26/05/21 ···
We can help her with rations

@khaanachahiye

💬 2   🔁   ♡ 4   ↑

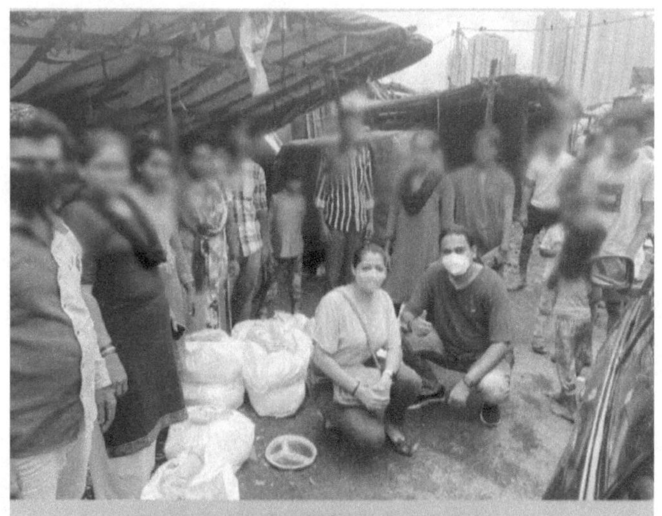
Way to spend your
Sunday
@khaanachaahiye

@khaanachahiye

As I mentioned before, what will remain closest to my heart was the work done by NIHAM Institute and its students during the pandemic.

This was a recent drive to distribute rations to the needy on 29th August 2021 in Bandra, Khar & Khar Danda. A few sample pics:

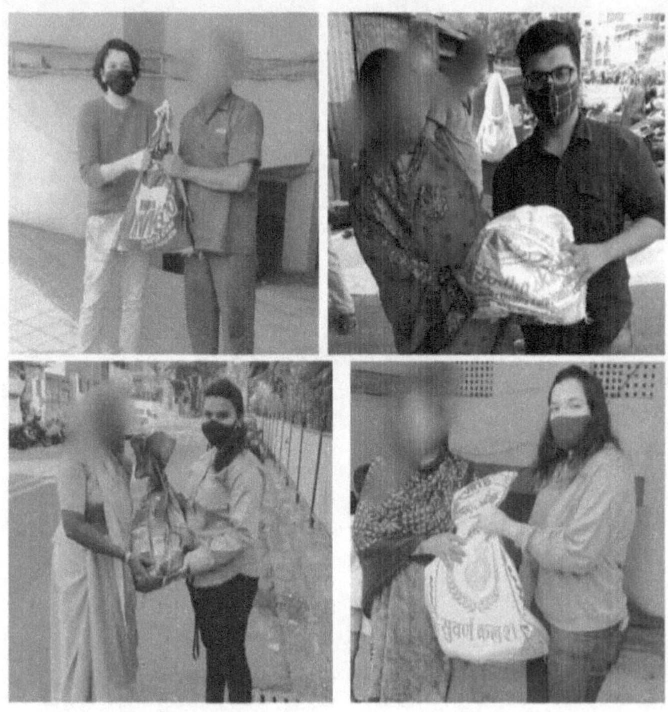

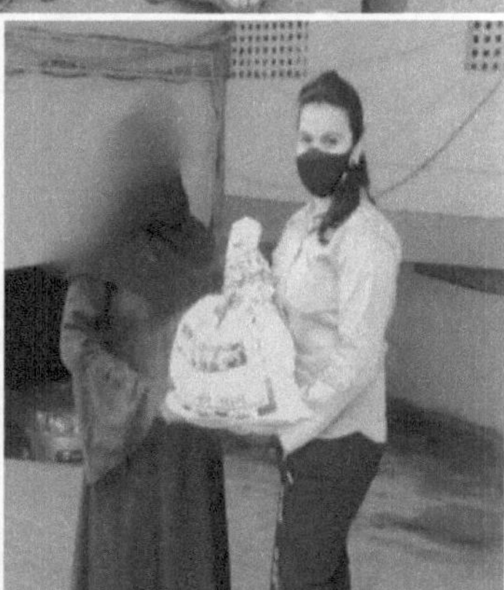

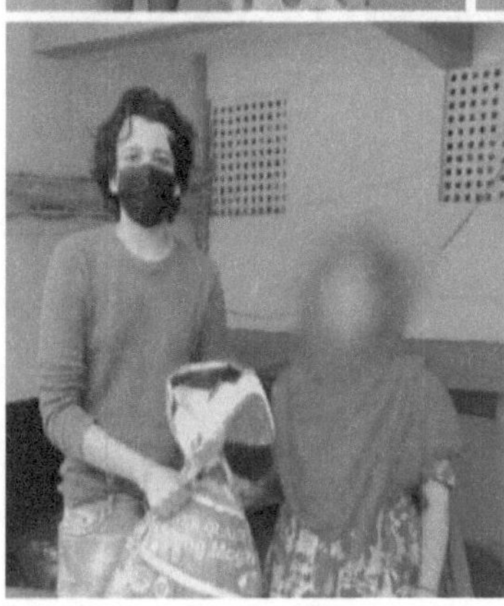

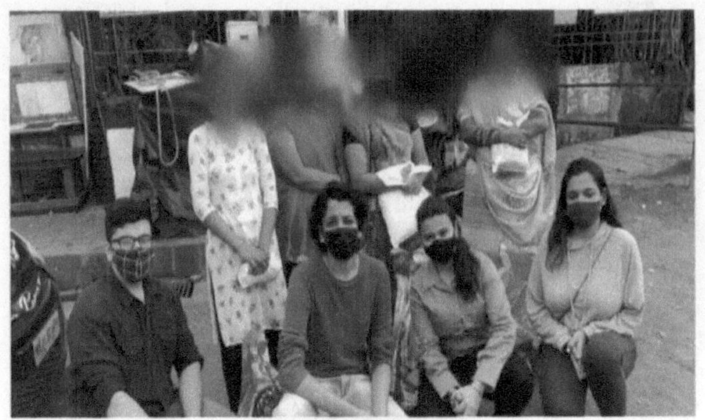

Ever since the second wave of the pandemic started, the healthcare system in India has been teetering on the brink, with many hospitals unable to handle the relentless inflow of patients whilst also running short of beds, oxygen cylinders and other essentials.

Healthcare workers say that amid crippling shortages of hospital beds, oxygen supplies and essential medicines, they are grappling to save patients. There is this sinking realisation that many lives could have been saved had there been enough beds, oxygen supplies, ventilators and other resources - if the healthcare system had been better prepared for the second wave.

Tanya*(Name changed on request), 26, a postgraduate doctor at the Nesco jumbo COVID-19 centre in Goregaon, Mumbai, describes the impact of the second wave succinctly, "It is definitely worse than last year. It's not a second wave - it's a tsunami that is happening."

Just as people were dropping their guards assuming that the worst was behind them, India was hit by a second wave of the pandemic, the magnitude of which is rendering its already precarious healthcare system more overburdened than ever. India has been reporting over two lakh cases a day in the past few days, making it one of the worst -affected countries in the world. News and social media are rife with harrowing accounts of overburdened hospitals, people scrambling to secure oxygen supplies and medicines, morgues piling up with bodies, and funeral pyres flickering away late into the night amid soaring deaths.

If migrants walking back home helplessly was the haunting image of the first wave, the drastic undersupply of oxygen cylinders is the blot of the second. We all read and saw news channels about how people across the country were dying due to lack of oxygen. Here's a fact: The Delhi government had formed a committee to look into Oxygen shortage Deaths during the second wave. But the Modi government rejected its formation. Why? Why not have an audit and know the truth, unless you're hiding something?

Even ghastlier, the Centre announced this on 20th July 2021:

Press Trust of India
@PTI_News

No deaths due to lack of oxygen were specifically reported by states and union territories during second COVID-19 wave: Govt

4:33 pm · 20 Jul 21 · PTI_Tweets

I couldn't stop myself from replying to this hysterical bullshit being fed to us:

Some more political *masala!*

As soon as the centre made this no lack of oxygen deaths statement, Chhattisgarh orders audit on deaths due to oxygen shortage, Says Centre is lying.

Speaking to NDTV, Chhattisgarh Health Minister TS Singh Deo claimed the central government never asked the state about the number of deaths due to oxygen shortage. *Abhi kis par bharosa kare yaar?*

Healthcare workers say that the new strain of the virus amid the second wave is more virulent and infectious, which is leaving more young and healthy people in critical conditions compared to before.

This time around, the situation was even more grim than last year as even the young are not spared. And the lung involvement is like really, really high. There were a lot of deaths being reported in the age group of 25 to 30 years.

Also, more than 60,000 children were infected in Maharashtra in just a month. "Children are definitely more infectious now than what we saw in the first wave", Tanu Singhal, a paediatrician and infectious disease specialist at Mumbai's Kokilaben Dhirubai Ambani Hospital, Told the *Hindustan Times*. He also said the severity of their illness had gone up. Some children had to be hospitalised in Mumbai for gastrointestinal infections, breathlessness and fever – all linked to the virus. They had to be put on intravenous fluids. Some even required steroids and oxygen support. I shudder to think of the possibility of a third wave, which experts have warned will effect children adversely.

Although Mumbai was better prepared than many other states across India, the fact remains that we are a densely populated city. As the spike in cases started rising rapidly, so did the panic for beds, oxygen and medicines. In fact many unworthy to live rascals started selling medicines like Remdesivir, Fabiflu and oxygen in the black market at astronomical rates. Some even fake!

This is where Mumbai united as one. Social media, especially Twitter for once proved useful for something more than just draining your phones battery. Many people started posting their problem and needs online. Requirements of beds, ICU's, oxygen, medicines, etc. Others like me and many more started to retweet them and amplify them by tagging those who could help.

Because the fact remained that at the peak, the city was at a panic mode and the authorities simply couldn't handle it alone.

Luckily for us, as I have repeatedly mentioned, we are blessed by angels. Far too many to name. Let me just name a few. Bollywood actor and real life hero Sonu Sood, Youngest MLA of Maharashtra (Congress), Bandra's Zeeshan Siddique, Working President of AAP Mumbai, Ruben Mascarenhas, Cabinet Minister Aaditya Thackeray (he tagged each tweet to the relevant BMC war room immediately for action to be taken), MP RajyaSabha (Shiv Sena) PriyankaChaturvedi, Equal rights crusader Harish Iyer, an equal rights activist (A godsend for many LGBTQ+), and countless such people out there, who worked tirelessly when the city needed them the most and saved many many lives from a possible disaster. I would like to share just a couple of twitter screenshots that show the same. They worked selflessly, without any political motive. The first image proves it. A Congress MLA and an AAP Leader working together. This is the new Mumbai, the young Mumbai. The future has hope. We should be grateful.

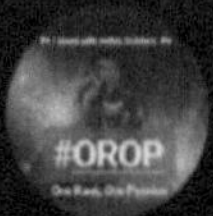

VISHAL DADLANI ✓ @VishalDadlani · 9h

A respected senior Classical musician needs help. Too frail to be hospitalised.

@rubenmasc @zeeshan_iyc

Name - Pt. Shankar Ghosh
Age - 81
Diagnosis- Covid positive
Need - Oxygen cylinder, flow meter & oxygen mask
Location - Mumbai
Contact - Mitul Soni
Mobile - +919930302730

♡ 9   ↻ 84   ♡ 123   ⇗

Zeeshan Siddique ✓ @zeeshan_iyc · 9h

Hi just read this, @rubenmasc are you covering this or should I?

♡ 2   ↻   ♡ 3   ⇗

Ruben Mascarenhas ✓ @rubenmasc · 8h

Bro, we have it covered, in touch with Mitul, have spoken to the supplier, figuring out the address. Will ping you if I need something or get stuck.

SHWETA SINGH
@shwets_singh

It is desperate call for a bed for my father #Lucknow #CoVID positive-oxygen levels dipping#SOS #any hospital contacts or any contacts please reach out #very very critical #COVID- and #DRDO is not taking direct admission

5:54 PM · 06/05/21 · Twitter for iPhone

491 Retweets **37** Quote Tweets **298** Likes

SHWETA SINGH @shwets_sin... · 20h
Replying to @shwets_singh
Resolved @ we finally got DRDO - have no words and gratitude for all the support that has poured in and that has made it happen

7 53

Zeeshan Siddique ✔ @ze... · 14/05/21
Like I said earlier the work you're doing is inspirational, happy to help in whatever way I can :)

 **bhumi pednekar** ✔ · 14/05/21

@zeeshan_iyc thank you for always helping me out 🙏 Really appreciate it

1 21 270

↺ harish 🏳 (he/she) Retweeted

Dhrstadyumn @Dhrstady... ·14/05/21 ···
@hiyer 1486+ lives saved, 2.55+ Lakh people reached Keep us going please share the verified resources from our handle:
Instagram:
instagram.com/thereisnoearthb
Twitter:
@ThereIsNoEarthB

harish 🏳 (he/she) ✔ @hi... ·13/05/21 ···
The best eid message you could get from someone. "Maa theek ho gayi"

Sar aapke halp se meiri maa thik ho gayi.
10:13

achha laga sunkar. Aasha karta hu, ke jald hi woh ghar aa jaayegi.
10:15 ✓✓

Eid mubaarak sar. 10:15

Eid Mubarak aapko aur aapke sab ghar waalon ko bhi.
10:16 ✓

💬 2   ↺ 4   ♡ 84   ⬆

Zeeshan Siddique ✔ @ze... ·12/05/21 ···
Happy to help mere bhai 🙏

Suraj Kanojia @Suraj... ·12/05/21

Big thank you to @Zeeshan_iyc bhai for providing 2 vials for Remdesivir at no cost
You are truly a blessing for people in disguise
@shams_iyc

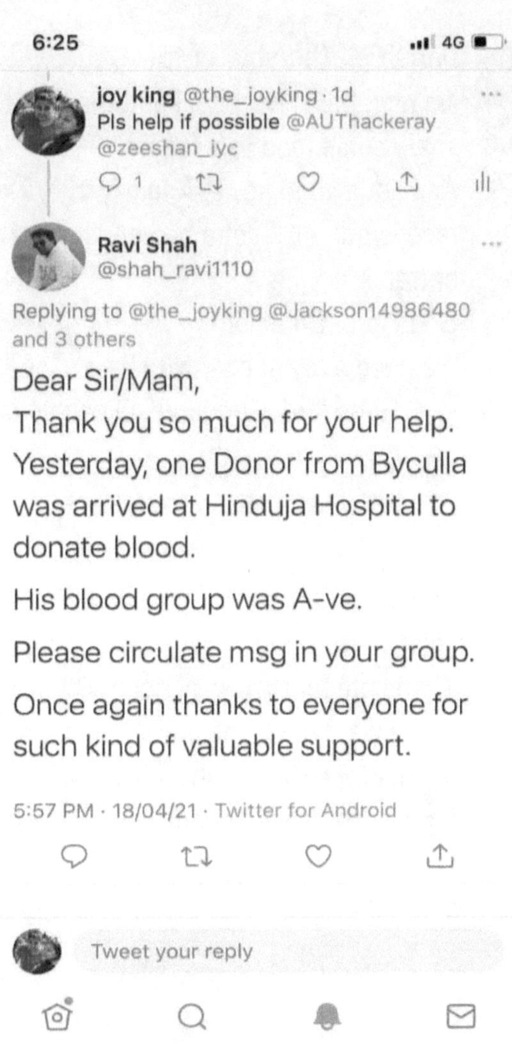
6:25
4G
joy king @the_joyking · 1d
Pls help if possible @AUThackeray @zeeshan_iyc
1
Ravi Shah
@shah_ravi1110
Replying to @the_joyking @Jackson14986480 and 3 others
Dear Sir/Mam,
Thank you so much for your help.
Yesterday, one Donor from Byculla was arrived at Hinduja Hospital to donate blood.
His blood group was A-ve.
Please circulate msg in your group.
Once again thanks to everyone for such kind of valuable support.
5:57 PM · 18/04/21 · Twitter for Android
Tweet your reply

harish 🏳️ **(he/she)** ✔ @hi... ·17/05/21 ···
I'm near MGM hospital kamothe now to share some food to a family.
And got a good news. A family of 5. 2 recovered. All 3 got a bed and are getting better
Good lord. Good lord.
We need a ray of positivity here. Good lord. Good lord. Good lord. O can't stop crying

💬 1   🔁 5   ♡ 34   ⤴

harish 🏳️ **(he/she)** ✔ @hi... ·17/05/21 ···
This entire family
 Complete family was serious. Thank you to the ward boys, the aayas, the nurses, the doctors, the rickshaw fellas who ferried the family, friends who donated and mom who cooked food all the time. I am so grateful.

💬   🔁 2   ♡ 13   ⤴

sonu sood ✔
@SonuSood

It takes me 11 hours on an average to find a bed in delhi.
&
It takes me 9.5 hours on an average to find a bed in UP.
Still will make it happen 🙏

6:04 PM · 30/04/21 · Twitter for Android

10.6K Retweets **510** Quote Tweets **96.2K** Likes

Some were unsuccessful. As was bound to be. Many stories of failure, despair, tears and agony. I'll share just one.

Sidin ✔ @sidin · 24/05/21
Thanks for everyone who tried (@rubenmasc @saviojoseph @priyankac19). He has passed away. Hugs everyone. Take care.

> 🧑 **Sidin** ✔ @sidin · 24/05/21
> Oh and my college mate who has the black fungus... situation is tough. Even the doctors are like better to raise money for his family than for his treatment. Sad days. Sad sad days.

💬 58   🔁 6   ♡ 130   ⬆

This one made me yell out loud. Helpless. Frustrated. Angry. Because thousands of these deaths could've been avoided. If they would get vaccines on time. They didn't. They died. Let's not mourn and forget. *Remember this. Vaccines were delayed.* That's the next chapter.

Chapter 4

Vaccination

Thank you readers for staying with me on this journey. Now let's talk about the biggest joke of the century. Until the pandemic struck, India was the world leader in vaccine production. Our pharmaceutical companies used to churn out 60 per cent of the vaccines needed for global immunisation programmes. *Yes, you read that right, 60%!*

The COVID-19 situation clearly shows that countries, and not pharmaceutical companies, need to play a pivotal role. This lesson must not be forgotten. Hence, it isn't India's Pharmaceutical Sector that has failed, it is Indian Government that has failed. What could have been an opportunity to turn into a global leader, turned into a downward spiralling tale of miseries?

On 16th January' 2021, a sanitation worker from Delhi -- Manish Kumar -- became the first person in India to receive the -19 vaccine jab after Prime Minister Narendra

Modi launched the world's largest vaccination drive on Saturday via video conference.

A total of 3,006 vaccination centres across all states and union territories have been virtually connected and 100 beneficiaries are being given the shots at each site on the first day.

"Everyone was asking as to when the vaccine will be available. It is available now. I congratulate all the countrymen on this occasion," said PM Modi.

The world's biggest vaccination drive was kickstarted shortly after PM Modi's speech with the jab being administered to Manish Kumar in Delhi's AIIMS.

The PM added that bad times for corona have begun as we have two made-in-India vaccines now.

Modi also harped on the fact that such a vaccination drive at such a massive scale was never conducted in history. There are over 100 countries having less than 3 crore population and India is administering vaccination to 3 crore people in the first phase only. In the second phase, we've to take this number to 30 crores, he noted.

Healthcare workers, both in the government and private sectors, are the first to get the shots.

The drive is being managed through CoWIN, short for Vaccine Intelligence Network, an online platform meant to facilitate real-time information of vaccine stocks, storage temperature and individualised tracking of beneficiaries for COVID-19 vaccine.

The drive will be held daily from 9 am to 5 pm, except on the days earmarked for routine immunisation programmes.

Union Health Minister Dr Harsh Vardhan had on Friday termed the country's vaccination drive as the "beginning of the end of COVID-19." He had also urged people to trust the indigenously manufactured vaccine, saying the government has given emergency use approval after proper scientific scrutiny.

Two companies are producing COVID-19 vaccines in India. Serum Institute of India, based in Pune, is working with AstraZeneca to produce Covishield; Bharat Biotech, based in Hyderabad, has taken a manufacturing licence from the Indian Council of Medical Research (ICMR) to produce Covaxin.

To begin with, why was only one company (Bharat Biotech) chosen for technology transfer. Including more companies could have boosted the process. Basic common sense!

Secondly, why choose a platform like CoWIN? I understand PM Modi's fascination with the concept of 'Digital India', but the truth remains that almost 70 percent of India is rural. They struggle with access to electricity, water roads, transport & everything else that a citizen is entitled to. Where the hell are they going to get access to high speed internet and computers/laptops/smartphones?

In fact, taking a dig at the Centre's argument that the poor and marginalised can lean on friends to register online for vaccination, the Supreme Court of India has said even the digitally literate are finding it hard to get vaccine slots on CoWIN.

Yeah, so coming back to the topic of the much awaited vaccination drive which was initially launched on 16 January' 2021 for frontline workers and other necessary candidates, it was announced that registrations for senior citizens would begin from 1st March 2021. Not for *ALL CITIZENS*, but only for those who were in the age group of 60 and above. 45 and above, if you suffered from co-morbidities.

Health Minister Satyendar Jain said that 308 centres were set up at 192 hospitals for vaccination. "There are 12-15 lakh people belonging to the age group of 60 and 2-3 lakh are from the age group of 45-59 with co-morbid conditions," he said. *Now consider this.* The population of Mumbai is roughly over 20 million. So just calculate the numbers.

Now let's ask ourselves a question. Who decides which life is more important? And mind you, this isn't a question that only I'm asking, it's being asked by the honourable court to the Union government regarding their vaccination policy. Does a citizen whose age is 60+ automatically become more important to save than someone who is 40? I figure out that if you ask a son if he wants to save his father or himself first, he is bound to say vaccinate my father first. But try asking the same question to the father. I assure you the answer will be different!

Why was this done? Simply because India didn't have enough vaccines. It was a result of the government's failure to procure the necessary number of vaccinations, in spite of sufficient time at hand. As a result they had to discriminate and decide whom to vaccinate first and whom to keep waiting. Hence, the rise of cases in the age group of 18 to 44 years during the second wave is not an accident or bad luck. Nor are the resulting deaths. It's the direct result of ineffective governance and hence deserves to be accountable for.

Another inexplicable thing is why they backed up on their statement and suddenly decided to increase the gap between the two doses of Covishield jabs to 3 to 4 months. They tell us it's more effective. *Really?* I've got a feeling it's just buying time to vaccinate everyone with at least the first jab.

And once vaccinations started for the age group of 18-44 years in May, the situation even worsened. Government hospitals were out of vaccines for this age group. However, private hospitals had stock! India has to be the first country in the world where the private sector can procure vaccines but the government cannot.

The Union government had eventually agreed on 3rd August 2021 as published in the National Herald, stated that it does not have data on the vaccines procured by private hospitals throughout the country, raising the question of how the government was following its own guidelines of procuring 25% of the vaccines for private hospitals and 75% of vaccines for the states and union territories.

This information was disclosed in a response from the Ministry of Health and Family Welfare (MoH & FW) to queries asked by RTI activist Kanhaiya Kumar using Right to Information Act. Keeping aside my reservations *(no pun intended;))* about Mr. Kumar, I'd like to thank him for getting the Union Government to accept their fault. *(I'm being decent here by only using the word 'fault').*

What a joke! Only if it were funny. Because as we saw later, most of the cases in the second wave were in this very age group. Vaccines were simply not available. The government however was busy doing PR and our CM was excited on reaching 2 crore jabs on 18th May 2021. It simply wasn't fast enough for a city like Mumbai. I'd like to share my reply to that particular tweet.

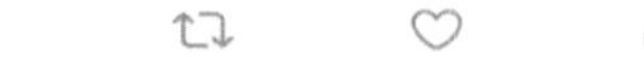

The US and UK decided to book and buy vaccines for the entire country in the middle of 2020. The government of India decided to do that in June 2021, that too after months of pressure from opposition parties and numerous times of humiliation in the Supreme Court. That is the reason why a uniform vaccine policy couldn't be rolled out.

Add to that the fact that the Centre had the nerve to say that *health is a state matter*. It's a freaking pandemic. The nationwide problem. Hence, the Centre's responsibility. Simple logic.

Next comes the matter of price. Initially, vaccines were free in Government hospitals and capped at 250 at private ones. Acceptable. After the 18-44 drive started, things went out of control. Some centres like Apollo and Hiranandani started charging upto 1800 rupees per shot! All this, while no doses were showing available in the government run hospitals. Why do we have to pay? Vaccines should be provided free to all. *Period*. The right to health is a guaranteed fundamental right for an Indian citizen, who also possesses a right to free vaccine as it is a sub-set of the right to life which is guaranteed by our Constitution.

The Union Governments stand was that they would procure and supply vaccines to states for the age group of 45 and above, but left the states to fend for themselves to procure vaccines for the age groups of 18-44. Which as we all know is the wide majority of the population. How is that fair? How is that even possible? The Co-Win (*Or Lose*) app was a joke. More like a fastest fingers first. Especially in the 18-44 category. I tried determinedly many days and than like you should do with all bad habits, just gave it up. Finally on June 12th 2021, my housing society arranged a vaccination drive in partnership with a private hospital, where we got a jab of Covishield each for Rupees 750/-. What about the unprivileged?

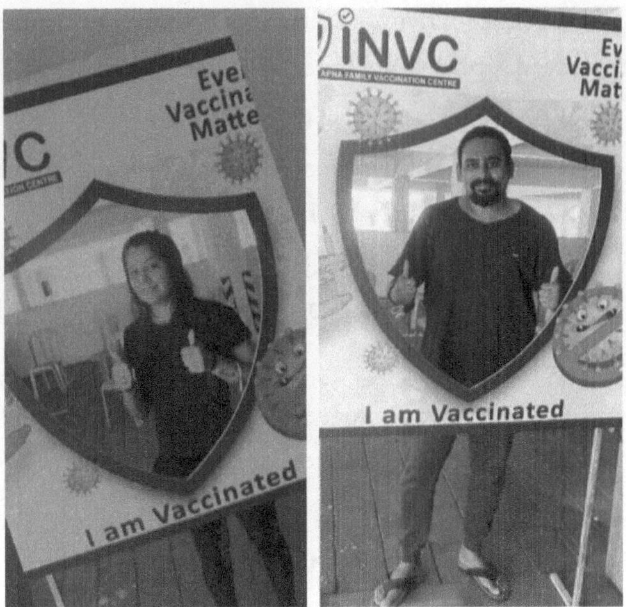

My wife and I breathing a sigh of relief after getting our 1ˢᵗ jab after 104 days of trying!

Did we have to beg for polio vaccines? Then why so for? Did we have to go all digital app's bat shit crazy for any previous disease that hit the nationwide? Then why so this time? Finally, after being cornered from all sides and the Supreme Court, the Prime Minister of India on June 7ᵗʰ 2021 declared that the Union Government has decided to procure vaccines for the state governments as well. More importantly, he declared that the benefit of the free vaccination drive will be extended to the 18 to 44 age group as well.

In a belated move, on April 16, 2021, the government announced a plan to include three PSUs in the vaccine-making process:

- Haffkine Biopharmaceutical Corporation Ltd, Mumbai (a state PSU)

- Indian Immunologicals Limited, Hyderabad (a facility under the National Dairy Development Board)

- Bharat Immunologicals and Biologicals Limited, Bulandshahr (under the Department of Biotechnology).

Grants will be provided to upgrade these units.

The Union government has also decided to support Bharat Biotech to upgrade its facilities. All these steps are expected to double the current production capacity of the indigenously developed Covaxin by May-June 2021, and increase it nearly six to seven times by July-August 2021. Vaccine production is expected to go up from one crore doses a month in April 2021 to about seven crore doses in July-August 2021, and nearly 10 crore doses per month by September 2021. *A LITTLE LATE, DON'T YOU THINK?*

As of July 16th 2021, The Prime Minister was meeting chief ministers from Tamil Nadu, Andhra Pradesh, Karnataka, Odisha, Kerala and Maharashtra - the six states with the highest daily trends at this time. These have contributed 80 per cent of new cases and 84 per cent of deaths in the past week, he said.

On Tuesday the Prime Minister met with the eight chief ministers of the northeastern states.

"To stop the third wave of COVID-19 is absolutely necessary. We have a strategy in place - 'test, track, treat and teeka (vaccinate)'. You are all familiar with this approach and are well-versed in it. This must be a priority," Prime Minister Modi said today.

"If the situation is not brought under control, there may be trouble ahead," he told the state leaders, while also highlighting the need to increase testing.

As the current situation stands, Amid rising criticism of the Centre's vaccination drive, Union Minister Prakash Javadekar, on 28th May 2021, said India will vaccinate its entire population by the end of this year.

I choose to be hopeful. Keeping my fingers crossed. For the millions of Indians who are yet to get even the first jab of any vaccine. And for everybody else whose wellbeing, financial needs, and most importantly, life is at stake. Especially since the WHO has categorically gone on record on 17th July 2021and stated that we are on the verge of a third wave, with multiple variants of , mutating and spreading rapidly. So, I hope that Mr. Javadekar's commitment of vaccinating a country of 1.4 billion people with 2 doses by December is kept true. Although, going by past experience, a bit skeptically.

Please allow me to share the reason for my skepticism. The current rate of vaccination is 4 million doses a day as per data available for June -July 2021. At this rate, we will get fully vaccinated not by this December but probably by the December 2022. So we will have to face a few more waves, lockdowns, joblessness, businesses getting shut, increasing poverty, declining GDP and yeah, lakhs of more deaths. The *ONLY* way to prevent this is by ensuring vaccination for maximum in minimum time. This needs to be our countries priority number one right now. Everything else can wait.

माझी **Mumbai**, आपली **BMC** ✓ @... ·5h ···
BMC Commissioner @IqbalSinghChah2 received the 'Mumbai Ratna Award' at the hands of Honourable @maha_governor Shri Bhagat Singh Koshyari for being an architect to the internationally acclaimed Mumbai Covid fight model.

(1/2)

PMO India and 9 others

♡ 45   ↻ 57   ♥ 569   ↑

But we in India, are habitual chest thumpers, number misinformers, and what not. Let's see an example of that. On July 19' 2021, while the city is still in the midst of a mini lockdown, The BMC commissioner gets felicitated!

Mumbai Fight model? Really? With a budget of almost 39,000 crores, the BMC has more funds at their disposable than some entire states of India. That's a fact. I'm not a naysayer, but how can you do PR activities, glorification and hand out awards when you have shut down peoples livelihoods. We are still asked to shut down all non essential shops establishments at 4 pm. Shut entirely on Saturdays and Sundays. People are crying out for rations. The threat of an imminent third wave looms overhead. These awards should be reserved for once the job is done. It's not even *half* done.

Let me give you another example of how well Mumbai's vaccination drive is being managed. Just two days after the BMC Commissioner received this award, the following was their twitter handle post:

Mind you, most private hospitals had stocks to *'sell'*. I'm confused whether to call it a *shame* or a *scam*.

And you know what, here's what the BMC said the next day:

Speak about incompetence. And yeah, further elaborating on incompetence:

BREAKING NEWS: To validate my previous skepticism about the vaccination drive for the adult population of entire India being completed by December end as was claimed by Union Minister PrakashJavadekar on 28th May 2021, here is an update issued on 23rd July'2021:

No Fixed Deadline For Completing Vaccination Drive In India: Govt Tells Parliament

ABP News Bureau

Last Updated: 23 Jul 2021 10:26 PM (IST)

The statement comes two months after the now Union Human Resource and Development Minister Prakash Javadekar said that India's vaccination will be completed before the end of 2021.

In the USA, CNBC published on June 8th 2021 that almost no one who has been vaccinated is being sent to the hospital or dying from the coronavirus, White House officials said. As more people get vaccinated against -19 in the U.S., a vast majority of hospitalisations and deaths are occurring among people who haven't yet gotten a shot. "Virtually all COVID -19 hospitalisations and deaths in United States are now occurring among unvaccinated individuals," White House coronavirus response coordinator Jeff Zients said at a press briefing. He said cases will continue to rise, especially among unvaccinated people, particularly as the delta variant takes hold in the U.S. "The bottom line is there's simply no reason that anyone 12 and older should be severely impacted by this virus," Zients said.

Thankfully, India too, has no realised that it's not just the 'adult' population, but the 'entire' population that needs to be vaccinated. Children need to go back to their schools, come home safe and not infect their grandparents and other children. While the US has already started trials on babies 6 months and older, India has finally awoken.

Children in India can start getting vaccinated by September, AIIMS chief Dr Randeep Guleria told NDTV this morning. "As early as September, we should see children being vaccinated," he said, adding that Pfizer, Bharat Biotech's Covaxin and Zydus shots should be soon available for children. This vindiacates what many like me have been going on and on about on social media that the numbers feeded to us our wrong. The math is incorrect. We need to consider our 'entire' population and then calculate the percentage vaccinated fully. Many got trolled for pointing out the Centre's flaw. To all those trolls, I wish to take this opportunity to extend you my polite middle finger. *No offence.*

At this time almost 50% of the citizens of the US are fully vaccinated. Almost 70% over the age group of 18+ had received at least one jab each. As of July 2021 over 52% of UK is also fully vaccinated. Hell, they've even opened night life! Yes, cases are rising, but fatalities are far, far lesser!

Rajdeep Sardesai ✔ @sardes... ·45m ···
UK opens for night life despite having 631 positive reported cases per million per day and climbing which is 22 times that of India at 28 positive reported cases per million per day and falling. The diff? Vaccination: over 52% of UK is FULLY vaccinated and only 5.7 % in India

💬 197   ↻ 88   ♡ 599   ↑

Have you ever wondered why Pfizer, Moderna, J&J, Sputnik and other top international vaccine manufacturers were not getting approved in India all this while? *When we really needed them. Badly.* I've got an opinion. I might be wrong, but I'm willing to go out on a limb here that it's because of corruption in Indian import policies and licensing procedures. Which obviously these companies didn't succumb to. And who paid the price for it? As always, the common Indian man. Because his life is just a number. A number that can be counted, discounted, and played political blame games upon.

In fact, these foreign vaccines should've been purchased long back, even if we had to pay double the price. Even triple. This wasn't a time to bargain! *It's not vegetables, it's life saving vaccines, you morons!* It could've saved so many lives. Eventually, we would've recovered the money spent on importing vaccines by bringing back normalcy to our lives. No lockdowns would mean more business, more employment, better economic stability, more tax revenue and eventually growth in the GDP.

What makes it even more important to source as many vaccines as possible, at any cost required, is a recent case study published in The Lancet journal. The researchers from University College London (UCL) in the UK noted that if the antibody levels of those injected with Pfizer and AstraZeneca (Covishield in India) vaccines drop at an alarming 50% in upto 10 weeks post receiving both dozes. This means a higher risk of vulnerability to any new variants that may arise. Hence, there is a high chance that we all may require a third powerful 'booster' shot. And here we are, where only 6% of the nation is fully vaccinated.

Even as lately as 31st July 2021, the WHO warned that the "Delta variant is a warning." Leaked internal CDC reports from the white house also said that the Delta variant has "Changed the war". This was later confirmed by Their President, warning that its mutating further is causing more hospitalisations and we need to be worried.

As we have already read before, my dear readers, if the mighty USA needs to be worried, than Mumbai, with our population density and all the math that we've already spoken, need to be doubly worried. *Seriously, start wetting your pants.*

Yeah, now let's come back to the point of accountability in post times.

As usual, after the dust settles there will be a lot of PR that India won, we defeated corona and a few lacs will be handed out to those families who lost lives due to the pandemic (*Only as per official statistics & after months of paperwork*). This money will come out of the PM CARES Fund, which we originally deposited in, anyways! So, Bottomline, the vast majority have short memories and all will be forgotten. We shall gloat in the greatness of our country and our Governments achievements. Those who raise their voices, shall be labelled leftists or anti-nationals. Worse still, if they belong to a particular religion, they will be asked to go to Pakistan.

Gandhi had once rightly quoted, that in India you cannot keep politics and religion separate. But let the narrative be different this time. Let's not have short memories. Let's not be classified as a third world country. Let's be united. Let's caste our vote not on the basis of religion and caste or regional divides. Let's not vote on memories of past prejudices. We need to drop this religious bias mentality if we don't want our country to suffer again. Never mix politics and religion. *That's plain stupid.* Our elected representatives are not gods. They are here to *SERVE* the country, to *SERVE* us. Let's vote for what democracy really stands. *FOR THE PEOPLE.* So that we, the people, don't ever have to face such pathetic situations again. So that human lives have at least some more value in the scheme of this country's governance. So that no more children die of hunger. So that no future pandemics so brazenly advertises our truth to the world. Because the sad truth is, COVID-19 didn't destroy our medical infrastructure. *It simply exposed it.*

Chapter 5

Road to Unemployment

Again, I would like to thank you, my dear readers for being with me through this tumultuous journey. Now that we have spoken about The what's, how's and if's of in Phase-1, Phase-2, The vaccination saga, lets stop for a moment and look at what happened to the common man, the average Mumbaikar, the normal Indian, in the meantime. The middle-class. Both Professionally employed, as well as self-employed.

To begin with, let's understand the importance of employment from a nations perspective. It is obviously important for a country's economic, social and environmental development process. It contributes to more spending power, higher productivity, higher GDP. And all such niceties.

Now let's understand the importance of employment from a family's perspective. Roughly 70% of India is rural, as we have already mentioned earlier. A lot of them have a family member or two working in cities like Mumbai or Delhi to earn their living and their family's sustenance as well. A study conducted a decade ago by BBC in India revealed that more than 90% of the country's labour forces were employed in the unorganised sector. I don't imagine the figure to have changed drastically even now, considering the ever increasing influx of migrant workers to metropolitan cities across the country.

Even if we forget the rural population, there are many middle class families also who have only one earning member. Just imagine their plight if he/she is jobless. Maybe they have savings and survive for a few months. Maybe they sell their gold. What after that? Banks aren't going to furnish loans to jobless people. As mentioned previously, a staggering 60% of the cases in the world that threw middle class families into lower class category are from India.

BBC News, Mumbai had reported on 6th May 2020 that India's unemployment rate was than at a record high of 27.1%, according to the Centre for Monitoring the Indian Economy (CMIE).

The new data shows India's unemployment figures are four times that of the US.

India doesn't release official jobs data (*No wonder why*), but CMIE data is widely accepted.

Unemployment hit 23.5% in April, a sharp spike from 8.7% in March. This is attributed to the lockdown, which brought most economic activity - except essential services such as hospitals, pharmacies and food supplies - to a standstill.

Scenes of desperate migrant workers, particularly daily-wage earners, fleeing cities on foot to return to their villages, filled TV screens and newspapers for most of April. Their informal jobs, which employ 90% of the population, were the first to be hit as construction stopped, and cities suspended public transport.

But protracted curfews and the continued closure of businesses - and the uncertainty of when the lockdown will end - hasn't spared formal, permanent jobs either.

Large companies across various sectors - media, aviation, retail, hospitality, automobiles - have announced massive layoffs in recent weeks. And experts predict that many small and medium businesses are likely to shut shop altogether.

A closer look at CMIE's data shows the devastating effect the lockdown has had on India's organised economy.

Of the 122 million who have lost their jobs, 91.3 millions were small traders and labourers. But a fairly significant number of salaried workers - 17.8 million - and self-employed people - 18.2 million - have also lost work.

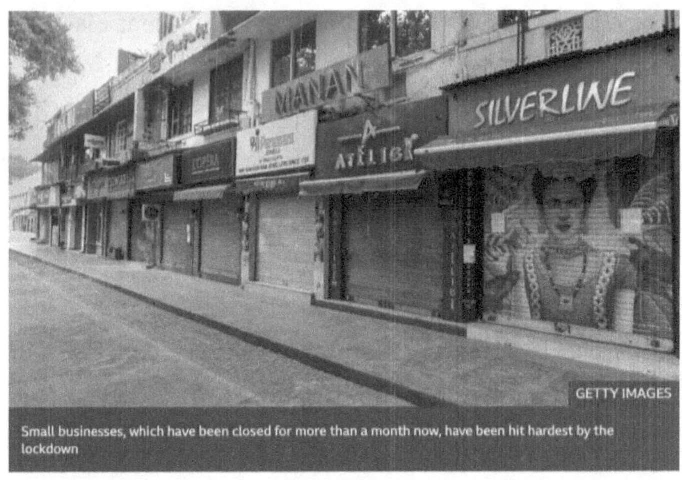

Small businesses, which have been closed for more than a month now, have been hit hardest by the lockdown

But the economic fallout of this unprecedented lockdown has been dire. Businesses have closed, unemployment has risen and productivity has fallen.

India's growth engine was actually sputtering well before the threat of outbreak arrived. Once one of the fastest growing economies in the world, its growth slowed to 4.7% last year - the slowest level in six years.

Unemployment was at a 45-year high last year. Industrial output from the eight core sectors at the end of last year fell by 5.2% - the worst in 14 years. Small businesses had only just begun to recover from the controversial 2016 currency ban that came as a body blow to the cash-consuming informal economy.

Now, experts say the coronavirus outbreak is likely to further cripple the already frail economy.

In the second wave in May 2021 data from the Centre for Monitoring Indian Economy (CMIE) show that unemployment rates in the country are slowly moving back to the record highs of June 2020 when there was a national lockdown.

Unemployment rate for the week of May 16 2021 shot up to 14.45 per cent on an all-India basis. For urban areas, it was higher at 14.71 per cent, while for rural areas it was a tad lower at 14.34 per cent, according to CMIE data. This is the highest since the week of June 7 last year, when the all-India unemployment rate was 17.51 per cent.

"By 2017-18, the unemployment rate was at a 45-year high. The pandemic has magnified this problem," said Santosh Mehrotra, labour economist and retired JNU Professor.

Till now, the second wave has hurt self-employed persons as well as informal workers in urban areas, which is also evident from reverse migration of many going back to their villages.

Microfinance players have been flagging the impact on incomes in the hinterland, as infections have soared in rural areas with almost no economic activity taking place in several pockets.

Let's talk about the key points of the 'Relief package' that was provided by the Government of India.

⋏ Rs. 2000/- to farmers from an annual pay-out to 'tide-over' the situation. Dear readers, please understand, this was their peak season. The new crop was ready – waiting to be sold. But prices had dropped drastically because there were no buyers due to the lockdown! The agriculture industry contributes over 250 billion $ to our GDP. I remember since childhood our school textbooks used to teach us *'Jai Jawaan jai Kisaan'* Is this how we repay our farmers and their families? Only 2000 rupees for an entire month? I strongly disagree. It's way too less.

⋏ India had announced a 20 lakh crore stimulus package. This works out to roughly 10% of our GDP. Just to compare, the relief package announced by Japan at the same time, in a far less dire situation was 21% of their GDP. Minus the corruption at various levels.

⋏ As part of the Rs 1.70 lakh crore Pradhan Mantri Garib Kalyan Package (PMGKP), the government announced free wheat or rice plus pulses to poor. Okay. Announcing something amounts to absolutely nothing. Delivering it is what matters. As we read earlier, thousands of villagers were stuck in other cities as immigrant labourers and daily wage workers. They became jobless overnight. They *didn't* receive their rations. The government should have cared more. Should have thought more. They could've deployed the military or a special task force to ensure fair delivery of promised money and ration to all the needy. They didn't.

"No-one will be allowed to go hungry," Finance Minister Nirmala Sitharaman said while announcing the package. *She failed.* As proved in the earlier chapters, if it hadn't been for hundreds of NGO's and social workers, not only would thousands of families go hungry, thousands would've died of hunger. In spite of all our efforts, many have still lost their lives of hunger and poverty.

So, is India's relief package enough?

Experts say it's a drop in the ocean compared to bailouts in countries such as the US, China and even Singapore. They say India now also needs a larger stimulus package soon to help businesses weather this extraordinary crisis.

As per an article published in the Financial Express on July 16th 2021, Urban men lost more jobs than women during the second wave of -19, implying a complete loss of livelihood for millions of households, according to the Centre for Monitoring Indian Economy (CMIE).

The most disproportionate loss of jobs because of the first wave of COVID-19 was among urban women, CMIE's MD and CEO Mahesh Vyas said in his analysis.

He said urban women account for about three per cent of total employment, but they accounted for 39 per cent of total job losses in the first wave of the pandemic.

Of the 6.3 million jobs lost, urban women accounted for a loss of 2.4 million, Vyas noted.

However, during the second wave, urban women suffered the least loss of jobs, he stated.

The burden of job losses has shifted to men and during April-June 2021, a disproportionately higher loss of jobs was incurred among urban men.

"Urban males account for about 28 per cent of the total employment in India. They accounted for a lower 26 per cent of the loss of jobs till March 2021. But, in the quarter ended June 2021 their share in total job losses was higher at 30 per cent," he pointed out.

Usually, urban male jobs are the better quality jobs and their disproportionate loss could imply a greater fall in income than witnessed so far, he said.

It is also likely that women are often the second earning member of a household and the loss of jobs among women more often than not implies a fall in income but not a complete loss of income, Vyas opined.

"But, a loss of job among men often implies complete loss of livelihood. This greater loss of urban male jobs is worrisome," he added.

As we spoke earlier, my dear readers, this has affected entire families and drove mass scale of middle-class to the brink of poverty and disparity. I know some of them are getting jobs elsewhere. Or maybe work from home options. Sometimes, later re-hired by their previous employers. But in almost all these cases, they have to settle for lower wages. Which drastically affects their standard of living. After all the government is doing nothing to reduce interest on loans, electricity bills seem to be increasing in Mumbai every passing month, school feels remain exorbitantly high, etc. How do these people survive? Mumbai, as India's financial capital, drastically needs an economic revival. I know I've repeated this for the second time in this book, but no number of repetitions are enough to drive home the point of how necessary this agenda is! The healthcare battle is lost, but the wealth care battle can still be saved. Household expenses is a vicious circle that never ceases to stop and grow.

The automobile industry, a key indicator of a country's economic growth, has also been forced to hit the brakes - experts are estimating losses of nearly $2bn.

The formal Sector has been largely insulated.

Staffing agencies indicate that many formal sectors such as IT continue to do well.

Suchita Dutta, Executive Director, Indian Staffing Federation, said there have not been job losses till now and some amount of hiring continues to take place in sectors such as IT, FMCG, deliveries, Pharma and Healthcare.

"The formal sector is well protected. Jobs are safeguarded, some hiring is happening. The January to March quarter had given a lot of hope with positive signs of recovery. The April to June quarter could however, be slow," she noted.

Amit Vadera, Assistant Vice-President – Staffing, Team Lease Services, also said that this time around organisations are better prepared to handle the lockdowns. In metro cities, hiring is happening in e-commerce, FMCG, telecom, but overall it has slowed down," he said.

But the industries that have been hit the worst are probably the tourism, hospitality and aviation sectors. And I will be talking about these two sectors at length in my next chapter, it being my area of expertise, my profession as an educationalist, and most importantly, my passion.

Chapter 6

How the Tourism, Aviation and Hospitality Industry Came to a Standstill

Once again, my dear readers, accept my thanks for staying with me through this book. We are on the last leg of this journey.

Let's note some important facts about the aviation industry in India. (Pre-COVID-19 statistics)

1) The aviation sector alone in India contributes $72 billion to our GDP and provides millions of jobs.

- The Aviation Industry in India is the most rapidly growing aviation sector of the world.

- With the rise in the economy of the country and followed by the liberalisation in the aviation sector, the Aviation Industry in India went through a complete transformation in the recent period. With the entry of the private operators in this sector and the huge cut in air prices, air travel in India were popularised.

▲ The growth of airlines traffic in Aviation Industry in India is almost four times above international average

▲ Aviation Industry in India has placed the biggest order for aircrafts globally.

▲ Aviation Industry in India holds around 69% of the total share of the airlines traffic in the region of South Asia.

▲ Up to 100% of NRI investment is allowed by the means of automatic approvals pertaining to the domestic air transport services

▲ In January 2020, IndiGo became first Indian carrier to have an aircraft fleet size of 250 planes and became the first airline to operate 1,500 flights per day.

▲ AAI plans to invest Rs. 25,000 crore (US$ 3.58 billion) in next the five years to augment facilities and infrastructure at airports.

▲ India's aviation industry is expected to witness Rs. 35,000 crore (US$ 4.99 billion) investment in the next four years. The Indian Government is planning to invest US$ 1.83 billion for development of airport infrastructure along with aviation navigation services by 2026.

Before the pandemic, India was one of the fastest growing aviation markets in the world. The domestic aviation sector witnessed double digit growth for five consecutive years from 2014-15 to 2018-19. In terms of domestic passengers handled, India is currently the third largest country in the world. Between 2009 and 2019, India contributed 5.9% to the global growth in passenger traffic making it a third largest contributor in the world.

The Aviation sector directly and indirectly contributes immensely to the economy. As per Oxford Economic analysis, the air transport sector in India directly contributes 3,90,000 jobs and indirectly supports over 5,70,000 jobs across different supply chains. Additionally, air transport facilitates tourism and investment into India. Foreign tourists arriving by air in India are estimated to support an additional 6.2 million jobs. Overall, the aviation industry contributes $35 billion annually to India's GDP. (*Screwed! Most of them, Screwed!*)

According to IATA Report, the average domestic fares in India have fell by 70% from their 2005 levels (after adjusting for inflation). India's ranking in Travel and Tourism Competitiveness Index has improved from 52nd in 2015 to 34th in 2019 reflecting a conducive policy environment. On the economic front, increasing size of India's middle class, growth in cross-border trade, development of world class airports, declining fuel prices and capacity expansion of low-cost carriers (LCCs) have been the driving factors. From merely 5 million LCC seats in 2004, airlines in India presently offer more than 135 million LCC seats.

However, COVID-19 has changed everything.

With the outbreak of COVID-19 pandemic, the outlook for the aviation sector has changed. According to Airports Council International (ACI), the global air passenger traffic is expected to decline by 60% during 2020 as compared to 2019. Even for the year 2021, the passenger traffic is expected to be down by 30% and global airline industry revenue down by 46% from their respective 2019 levels.

The aviation industry has suffered more than most as the pandemic destroys ticket sales and strips companies of cash. Airlines the world over have drastically cut back on flights due to border restrictions and a lack of appetite for travel, particularly internationally, because people are worried about contracting the virus and spending lengthy periods in quarantine.

The minimum estimate job-loss figure for airlines worldwide is 400,000 and covers pilots and cabin crew, who have found themselves on the front lines of the virus fight when they are at work. It includes planned cuts by U.S. carriers and was compiled from company statements, Bloomberg News stories and other media reports.

Job losses in related industries including aircraft manufacturers, engine makers, airports and travel agencies could reach 25 million, according to the International Air Transport Association. The hotels and lodging sector in the U.S. sees 7.5 jobs lost for every one in aviation. Airbus SE and Boeing Co. are cutting more than 30,000 positions.

Back home, the air passenger traffic in India is expected to shrink by 49% in 2020 as compared to 2019 (IATA). Various international agencies expect that the sector will take at least three to four years to achieve pre-levels. 2021 is a disaster.

It goes without saying, that if passenger traffic shrinks by almost 50%, (as per IATA estimates) in a country like India, the brunt of the effect is going to be felt in the Tier-1 cities. Delhi and Mumbai are the top two cities which receive the maximum passenger traffic in our country. Obviously, as a cascading result the job cuts were felt worst over here. Employees were asked to take pay-cuts. Some were asked to go on indefinite periods of LWP (Leave without Pay). Some were simply asked to resign.

All airlines cut staff salaries too to reduce their expenses while GoAir saw exits of several senior executives.

Even after job cuts/salary cuts during the first wave, Spicejet was still reeling so badly during the second wave, that in April 2021 it had to partially outsource some of its ground handling work to CelebiNas, a reputed Ground handling Agency from May 1ˢᵗ. 300 employees were immediately laid-off. Most of them were drivers and loaders. The employees also complained that they weren't paid their full salaries for over a year now, nor were they paid their statutory annual bonuses since 2019.

Some pilots of Spicejet even complained of pay-cuts of upto 85%! Now that's simply crazy, right?

The country's largest domestic airline IndiGo slashed its workforce by ten per cent on July 2020. responding to travel disruption.

I still vividly remember it was 14th April 2020. I was sitting near my balcony with my morning tea peeking outside my window where some families were enjoying lock down as they finally got time to spend together, some were enjoying their break. While I was in the mids't of these thoughts my phone rang. It was from an HR of a reputed ground handling agency (Name withheld). After we exchanged greetings, the first thing I was asked how are the other airlines doing? How much salary cut are employees being given?

The fact was that right from AGM, GM, Supervisor, Pilot, Cabin Crew, Ground staff and others were taking an approximate 25% or more pay cut! I was speechless.

Ground handling agencies with more than 2000 employees gradually came down to a mere 20 ground staff. Yes, you heard me right. *That's* how bad the Aviation sector was hit. Even other airlines like Indigo, Spicejet, Go air and Ground handling agencies like BWFS.

Few stories which I heard first hand like Mr ABC working as pilot with Go air had recently married another pilot and moved to Mumbai. Both lost their jobs, within a span of a few weeks.

Anyways, since Jet airways had shut operations in 2019, many employees were jobless and had finally landed a job with other airlines, only to be jobless once again.

How do you feel to be here while you dress up in your uniform and are about to leave for your duty and you receive an e-mail stating that due to the pandemic you are terminated with immediate effect and would be called in future incase we hire. Without a prior notice hundreds of employees lost their jobs in this manner.

Laid off from jobs, salary cuts, Air Canada, Delta, EK dissolved and operated only rescue flights,

Air France & KLM at one point of time were collectively working with 20 employees only. *Yes,* it really looked like one haunted airport.

CAPA (Centre of Asia Pacific Aviation (CAPA India) – a global aviation consultancy) tweeted on Tuesday:

"Industry conditions are such that one or more airline failures appear inevitable. Airlines have limited options to turn to for funding except their promoters, given that 3rd party investors will be reluctant to provide capital right now, and the government is *unwilling* to do so." *(Focus on the word UNWILLING)*

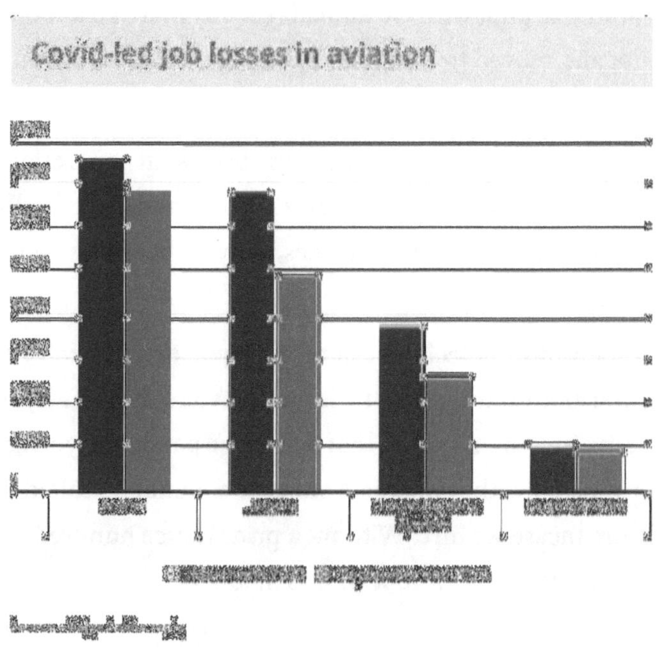

Same was the case with the travel companies. No tourists, no tourisms, lockdowns. Many small companies shut shop forever. Some simply fired their employees and waited for things to return to normalcy.

Mumbai alone has around 50 five star hotels, and many more four and three star hotels who are dependent on tourism to meet their room occupancy targets. They suffered the same fate.

The first lockdown was a kick in the gut for the restaurant industry. Hundreds of restaurants closed down. Thousands of employees were jobless. Some startup restaurants that had invested over a crore in their set-ups in malls were closed overnight. The stories are endless.

Thankfully, things were a bit better during the second lockdown because of delivery partners like Zomato and Swiggy. But the truth remains that the majority of the staff, the stewards, the restaurant hostess, the bartenders, they are still jobless.

Many of these employees who lost their jobs overnight were working with 'reputed' companies until just a day before. Many were financial contributors to their families expenses. Some were the sole bread earners. Almost everyone in todays age has some kind of overheads. Credit card bills, car loans, home loans and the likes. There's the punch. These people, unless they were careful enough to save up for bad times, were, in simple words, *screwed.*

Here is my honest opinion. The government, I won't point fingers to Centre or State, just that*OUR* government simply didn't care enough for thousands of such people. There could've been moratoriums granted in Metropolitan cities at least to people who furnished valid proof of losing their jobs and are unable to repay loans until they get re-employed.

You want 'Digital India' Mr. Prime Minister? All such employees have salary accounts linked to their Pan cards. Make linking Aadhaar cards compulsory for people who want to avail of moratoriums. *Ergo,* as soon as they get a job and start getting salaries, their moratoriums are stopped! This simple move could have saved so many families from bankruptcy!

This is what you use digitalisation, technology and money for. *(I'm pinching myself to not mention the Pegasus spying scam);)*

So many individuals financial status in the form of track records and borrowing capacity in the form of CIBIL scores are done and dusted. Because they didn't receive any financial aid.

As a direct result of your inaction, there will be low purchasing power in the middle class for the foreseeable future, which means less demand. In turn, less production. Less jobs. Long term affect on our economy, because of your short-sightedness.

Yes, RBI would have to circulate more currency after printing, thereby increasing inflation. That's your argument, right? *HELLO!* You *can't* talk about inflation when we Mumbaikar's are paying 108 rupees for a litre of petrol now, can you?! Inflation right now, to the average

Indian is like a thorny stick right up his butt! Even *you* can't screw it up more!

Getting back to jobs. The worst hit was probably the class of 2020. I can't comment on other industries, as some like IT enabled ones had the work from home option and many others likewise. I've provided my opinion based on statistics, facts and figures in the previous chapters.

However, I can say that for sure at least in the field of Aviation & Hospitality, as there are simply few to none job openings. At a time when these youngsters should've been preparing their interview pitch and honing their skills, getting acquainted with the realities of a first job, they have been sitting at home since over 15 months already and God alone knows for how much longer. Some who were from financially weaker backgrounds picked up menial jobs like delivery for Amazon/Flipkart/Swiggy/ Zomato, or whatever work from home opportunities were available.

We tried our best. Spoke to Senior HR's of various airlines, hotels, travel firms and embassies. Managed to save a few jobs. Managed to get some new students recruited as well. But there were simply not enough opportunities for everyone.

In just a matter of a few days, India's second most busiest airport (in terms of passenger traffic), turned into a haunted zone. The hustling bustling beautiful place was eerily quiet. With few passengers, and fewer employees. Never in my life have I encountered unemployment of this magnitude. Experts reckon its worse than the great Depression of 1929.

Just look at the following two images. The first is from July 2019 and the second is from March 2020. Stark difference, even though the outbreak had just begun!

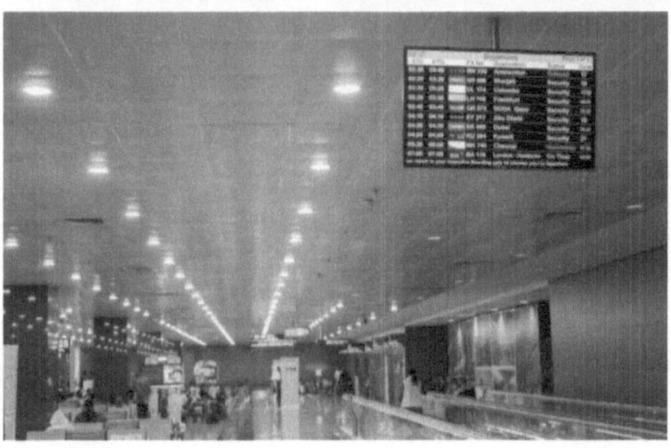

But all is not lost. Not *yet* at least.

The aviation industry has repeatedly shown the resilience to come back stronger, bolder and smarter from previous crises that have threatened to disrupt the status quo. There is a need for a sharp, rational and consistent approach to reforms to help the industry cruise at a newer and higher altitude and redefine its new normal. The changing geo-political scenario and impending power shifts globally also demand a swift and adroit approach. Expedient policy changes will be required to exploit the opportunity, accumulate strategic gains and create a better future.

There needs to be more joint ventures, collaborations, use of technologies like RFID tags, paperless check-in, green house concepts, solar powered airports, and many more things that can be effectively done to bring back normalcy.

Also, another good point is that travellers are itching to pack their bags. So once things are back to normal, we will definitely see a hike in flight occupancy. Business travellers might take their time, but leisure travellers definitely won't. *(Trust me, my wife has already made plans, planned venues, planned clothes, shopping, et al!)*

But most importantly, we are looking at the Government of India, under the leadership of the new Minister of Civil Aviation, Shri Jyotiraditya Scindia (in the recently reshuffled cabinet), to provide the much needed impetus that this industry needs. With Jet airways about to find its wings back again thanks to London based Kalrock Capital and UAE based businessman MurariLalJalan and also the proposed Navi Mumbai airport in the pipeline, and many such projects that have been announced, there is hope. *Serious hope.*

Please don't let us down again. Please don't turn a deaf ear and blind eye to the youth of the country again. Remember, you need us just as much as we need you. This is 2021. The next Indian General Election in 2024 is approaching. Fast.

In the meantime, let me share some WhatsApp screenshots that we had the unfortunate destiny to chat with some of our ex-students. This will give my readers an insight into the gravity of the on ground situation:

72% 11:22
What is this regarding? 15:41
Regarding airport job 15:52
RAM 78%
Genuinely ma'am I need a job 16:48
30 May 2021
Hello dear, I'm sorry Airlines aren't hiring. Some 5* hotels have started hiring. If vaccinations happen, job offers will be ur way soon. Keep following our social media pages. We will contact u as well. 11:43
Oky ma'am 12:04
But what is your social media I'd? 12:05
U have any kind of job ? 15:22
I'll do that 15:22
31 May 2021

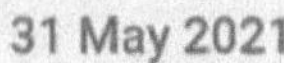

Type a message

71% 11:25

I'm sorry mam,I can't manage to arrange fee,I m promiseing,as soon will get job I'll start to pay fee EMI.
12:33

RAM 77%

Hop in this situation y will help me
12:34

He is ready to typing job also   12:35

+91 97693 67750
Hop in this situation y will help me

No issues I understand your situation. Don't worry about the EMI & things will get better soon. Take care
Thanks & Regards
16:00

+91 97693 67750
He is ready to typing job also

Shall speak to the concern person and update u in a while
16:01

22 May 2021

Type a message

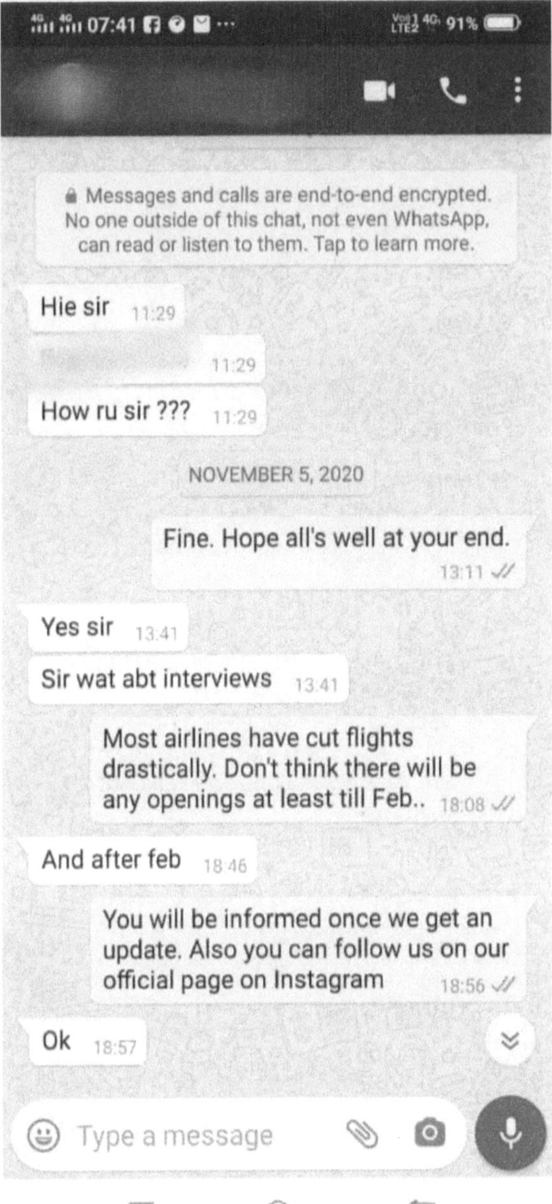
07:41
Messages and calls are end-to-end encrypted. No one outside of this chat, not even WhatsApp, can read or listen to them. Tap to learn more.
Hie sir 11:29
11:29
How ru sir ??? 11:29
NOVEMBER 5, 2020
Fine. Hope all's well at your end.
13:11
Yes sir 13:41
Sir wat abt interviews 13:41
Most airlines have cut flights drastically. Don't think there will be any openings at least till Feb.. 18:08
And after feb 18:46
You will be informed once we get an update. Also you can follow us on our official page on Instagram 18:56
Ok 18:57
Type a message

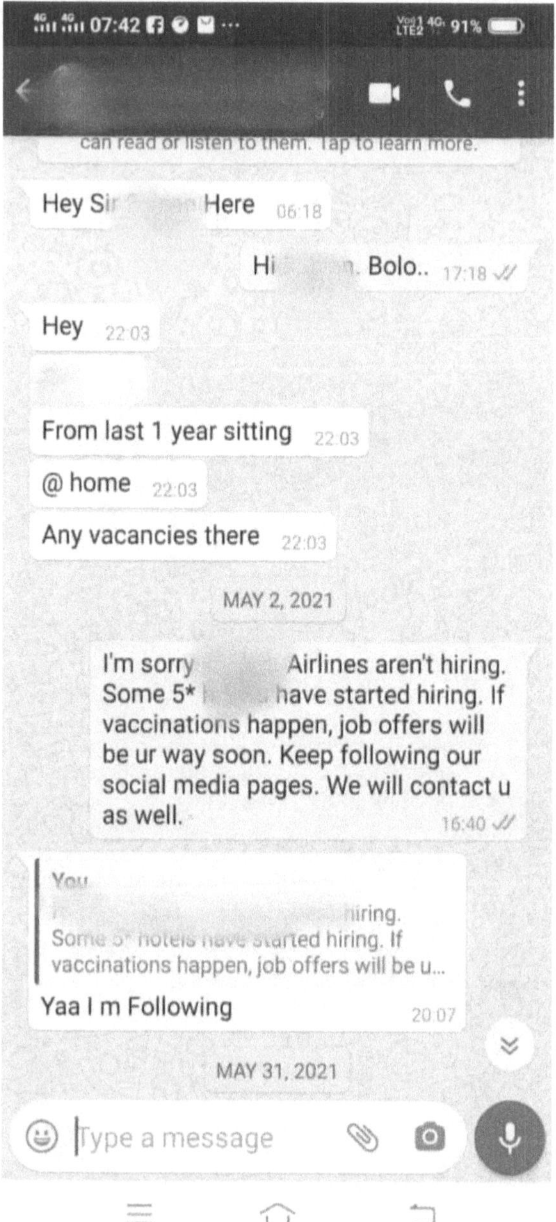
07:42
91%
can read or listen to them. Tap to learn more.
Hey Si   Here 06:18
Hi   . Bolo.. 17:18
Hey 22:03
From last 1 year sitting 22:03
@ home 22:03
Any vacancies there 22:03
MAY 2, 2021
I'm sorry   Airlines aren't hiring. Some 5*   have started hiring. If vaccinations happen, job offers will be ur way soon. Keep following our social media pages. We will contact u as well. 16:40
You
hiring. Some 5* hotels have started hiring. If vaccinations happen, job offers will be u...
Yaa I m Following 20:07
MAY 31, 2021
Type a message

think recruitment might start before
February
20:06

Alright mam   20:31

RAM
77%

22 May 2021

Hello Ma'am,

I completed my course in 2018   14:20

Is there any job openings ?   14:20

I'm sorry Airlines aren't hiring. Some
5* hotels have started hiring. If
vaccinations happen, job offers will
be ur way soon. Keep following our
social media pages. We will contact
u as well.
20:59

You
I'm sorry Airlines aren't hiring. Some 5*
hotels have started hiring. If vaccinations
happen, job offers will be ur way soon. K...

Alright, Thank you   21:00

Type a message

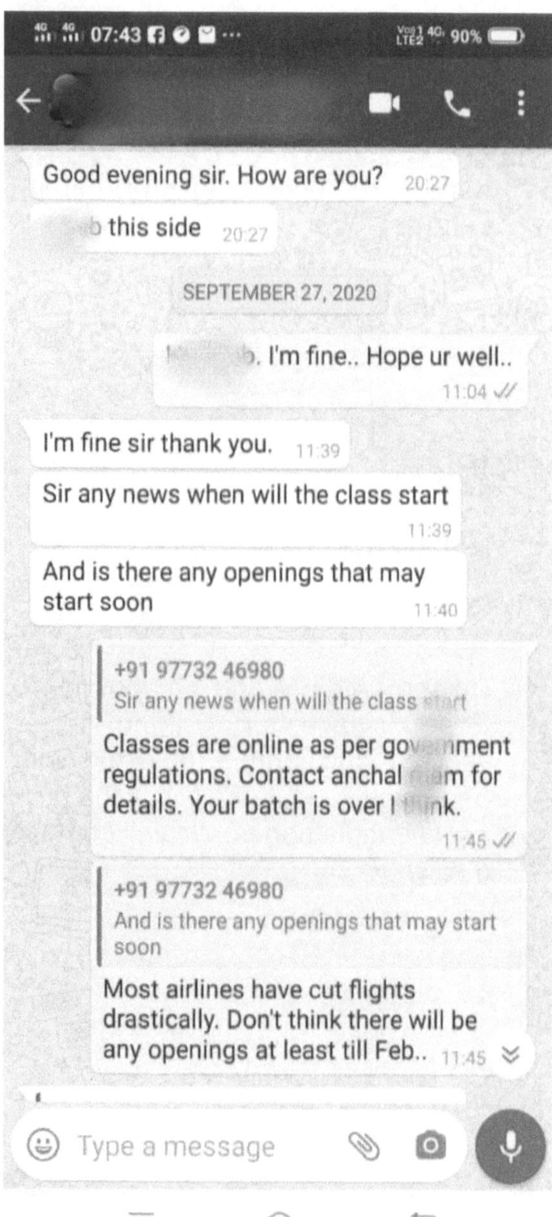
07:43
90%
Good evening sir. How are you?   20:27
this side   20:27
SEPTEMBER 27, 2020
. I'm fine.. Hope ur well..
11:04
I'm fine sir thank you.   11:39
Sir any news when will the class start
11:39
And is there any openings that may start soon   11:40
+91 97732 46980
Sir any news when will the class start
Classes are online as per government regulations. Contact anchal mam for details. Your batch is over I think.
11:45
+91 97732 46980
And is there any openings that may start soon
Most airlines have cut flights drastically. Don't think there will be any openings at least till Feb..   11:45
Type a message

4 January 2021

Hello ma'am
Maam it has been a year with no job in hand now its 2021 I have responsibilities please do something for my job please maam
16:55

Good evening, I'm sure you know it's almost been a year of pandemic there are no jobs....some of our students are still on leave without pay.. I understand your concern but none of our clients are hiring right now. As soon as we have requirements we will update on our official page please follow us for more updates. Please be patient this bad time shall pass.
21:25 ✓✓

Okay ma'am thank you so much that you can understand my concern
22:46

30 January 2021

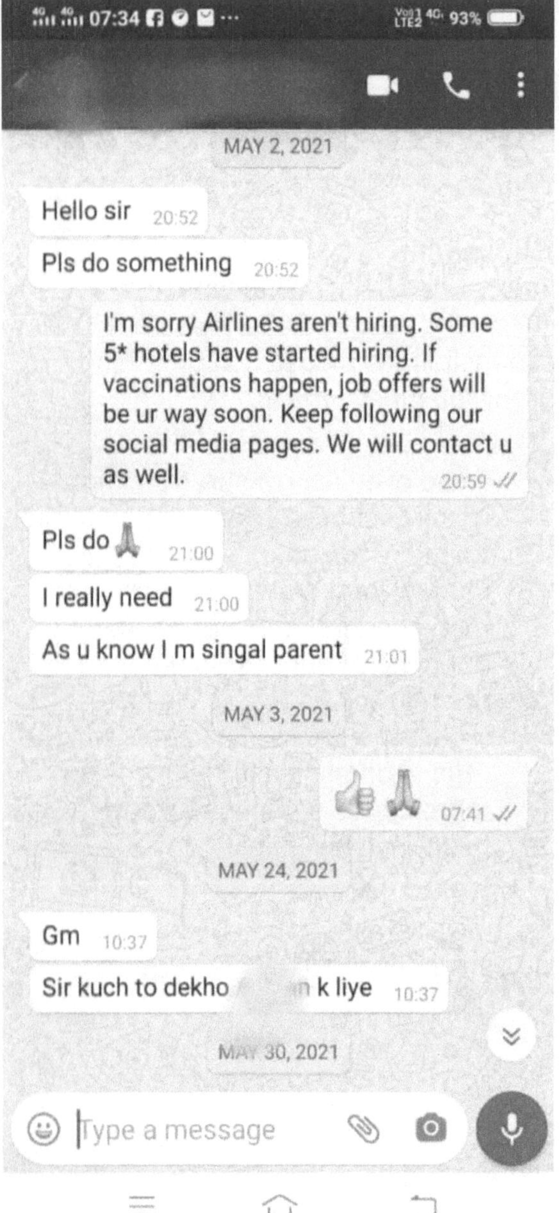
MAY 2, 2021
Hello sir 20:52
Pls do something 20:52
I'm sorry Airlines aren't hiring. Some 5* hotels have started hiring. If vaccinations happen, job offers will be ur way soon. Keep following our social media pages. We will contact u as well. 20:59
Pls do 21:00
I really need 21:00
As u know I m singal parent 21:01
MAY 3, 2021
07:41
MAY 24, 2021
Gm 10:37
Sir kuch to dekho n k liye 10:37
MAY 30, 2021
Type a message

Forgive me for my 'Gully boy' movie hangover. But here's a few lines from the song 'Azaadi' that aptly engulfs my fury over our Governments apathy towards the Generation X and Y's unemployment problems:

Bohot baithey chup chaap, Kya ghante ka insaaf
Desh kaise hoga saaf, Inki neeyat mein hai daag
Sirf karte rahenge baat, Alag Shakal wohi jaat
Vote milne par ye khaas, Phir gaayab poore saal

Haan mera bhai, hai toh noton ki sarkaar haina
Note se banate, apne beton ko yeh star hain na
Kitne bekaar kyun, yeh aapas mein jhankaar hain na
Baaki poora desh dubey, inki naiyya paar haina

Achhi vidya chahiye, achha khaasa maal dena
Nall mein paani chahiye, khade rele line mein na
Zameen apni, par note dikhakar sign lena
Drugs laye yeh, phir dhakel denge crime pena

Andekha kyun hai jaanke bhi
Sachchai mein tu sama kabhi

Achchai se tu kama kabhi

Iss gandh ko karna saaf abhi

Bolo Azaadi, Give Me Freedom!

Yes, It is so very true. We need our true *Azaadi*. We need freedom in the real essence. Freedom from corruption. Freedom from hunger. Freedom from religious persecution. Freedom of the press. Freedom of speech. Freedom of expression. Freedom to every student and adult to speak out what they feel, without the fear of being punished for no rhyme or reason. Freedom from forced poverty. Freedom from unemployment. Freedom from oppression.

The city of dreams is slowly seeing it's middle-class waning. It's either the shine and glitter of the rich, or the filth and despair of the poor, where their kids take to having '*ganja*' while still in school. We need our government facilities like the schools and hospitals to at least be 70% as good as their private counterparts.

We need no more deaths because of road accidents due to potholes in the Mumbai rains. We need safe drinking water from the tap. *Period*. BMC can't afford to provide it with their massive financial budget? Go back to school. Puri, a city in Odisha, recently became the first Indian city to achieve 24/7 quality drinking water supply. It adheres to quality standards of IS 10500. It will benefit the 2 crore tourists who visit the holy place annually, along with the locals. So don't rebuttal with the population answer. Where there's a will, you will find a way.

You know what friends, the problem is not the office bearers or the people in power. It's *US. WE.* We sit and watch things happening around us, sometimes pass a comment, and sometimes, let's face it, we just don't give a shit. It's time to change our attitude. *It's time we give a shit!* More than that. The buck stops here! It's time to take what is rightfully ours. What our forefathers died for, fighting foreign invaders right from the Mughals to the British, to pass it on to us. *AZAADI.* FREEDOM. Let's respect it, understand it & demand it. Together!

Let these two years of this deadly Global pandemic open our eyes. We owe it to the lakhs of people who lost their lives in this pandemic, and to the lakhs of their family members who are waiting for justice.

I'll end this book with a famous quote by Martin King Luther - "Our lives begin to end the day we become silent about things that matter."

Jai Hind! Jai Maharashtra!

Mumbai Meri Jaan!

References

The Times of India

India Today

DOWNTOEARTH.ORG.IN

Twitter

ANI

NDTV

BusinessLine

Business-standard.com

The Hindu

livelaw.in

Economic times

India times

cnbc.com

Financial Express

thehindubusinessline.com

deccanherald.com

cgdev.org

kpmg.com

National Herald India

Inspirational lines from The movies 'Rang De Basanti' & 'Gully Boy'

www.ingramcontent.com/pod-product-compliance
Lightning Source LLC
Chambersburg PA
CBHW031128250726
48655CB00002B/567